Structuring Paragraphs

Structuring Paragraphs

A Guide to Effective Writing

A. Franklin Parks

James A. Levernier

Ida Masters Hollowell

St. Martin's Press
New York

Library of Congress Catalog Card Number: 80–50641
Copyright © 1981 by St. Martin's Press, Inc.
All Rights Reserved.
Manufactured in the United States of America.
54
f
For information, write St. Martin's Press, Inc.,
175 Fifth Avenue, New York, N.Y. 10010

ISBN: 0–312–76865–6

Contents

Chapter 4: Methods of Development   49

Chapter 5: Achieving Coherence   **105**

Chapter 6: From Paragraph to Essay   **147**

Preface

As composition instructors in a variety of settings—the open-admission university, the private college, the state college, the technical school, and the community college—we have found that the most efficient way to teach the basic principles of good expository writing is to focus on the paragraph. Most college students, regardless of ability, are insecure about writing, and mastery of the paragraph is a less forbidding challenge than mastery of the complete essay. The essential skills of paragraph writing, however, are substantially the same as those demanded by the effective expository essay. Our experience has been that the student who can write a paragraph that is purposeful, coherently developed, and free of grammatical and usage errors is more than ready to tackle the essay when the time comes. Our book is not just "a paragraph book": we progress systematically through five chapters on the paragraph to two on the essay to complete what we call in our subtitle "a guide to effective writing."

Our method, both in the classroom and in this book, is to move step by step into the general-to-specific paragraph, introducing one principle at a time. Abundant examples and extensive exercises illustrate and explore the range of each concept. All of the examples and exercise passages are from students' work because we have achieved our best results encouraging students to emulate their successful peers. The design of the book and the wealth of example and exercise material offered give the instructor the freedom to adapt this program to the requirements of a particular class. The teacher who wishes to assign most of the exercises can structure an entire semester around the book. Another instructor might wish to focus on selected concepts and their accompanying exercises to complement other course materials.

Following Chapter 1, which introduces the student to the general-to-specific paragraph as an "essay-in-miniature," the text proceeds from smaller to larger units of exposition. Chapter 2 explains the topic sentence, which we divide into two components—the topic and the controlling idea. We present the topic as the subject of the paragraph and the controlling idea as "focusing words" that indicate what the writer wishes to say about the topic. Chapter 3 addresses paragraph unity and shows the student how to select and arrange sentences of primary and secondary support for the topic sentence. Chapter 4 explores six methods of paragraph development: example, definition, comparison and/or contrast, classification and division, cause and effect, and process analysis. Chapter 5, discussing coherence, deals with the ordering principles of time, space, and importance as well as with transitional devices and sentence combination. Chapter 6 shows the student explicitly how the skills acquired working with the paragraph apply to the essay. Here we concentrate on the 1-3-1 essay—that is, the essay composed of an introduction, three body paragraphs, and a conclusion. Chapter 7, the book's last, offers advice on the revision both of first drafts and of the essays after the instructor has read them. A checklist for revision is included.

As in any undertaking of this sort, we have incurred innumerable professional debts. Without the help of Daniel F. Littlefield, Jr., we might never have begun. We are similarly indebted to Dianna Denham Parks, whose encouragement carried us through the early stages of development. For technical assistance and manuscript typing, we should like to thank Sharon Ritchie. Nancy Perry and Ruth Anderson—among others at St. Martin's Press—made valuable suggestions. To our students, who let us know that we were on the right track and who supplied us with our writing samples, we owe the most.

A. Franklin Parks
James A. Levernier
Ida Masters Hollowell

Structuring Paragraphs

Chapter 1

Introduction

Much of the writing you will do, in college and throughout your career, is *expository*, and the quality of your work will depend on how well you have mastered the skills and concepts that are basic to good expository prose. Expository prose is writing that *explains:* your purpose may be to describe a process, define a term, or discuss an idea or a point of view. In college, you will frequently be asked to write essays, research papers, or reports. On the job, you may be required to prepare letters, briefs, memorandums, or other written material. The writing skills you will need to accomplish such assignments successfully include the ability to select a topic and limit it, to organize and unify your material, to develop your topic adequately, and to connect your ideas logically and smoothly.

One good way to acquire these basic writing skills is to start on the level of the paragraph, where the demands of length do not overshadow the need to improve the *quality* of your writing. Concentrating on the paragraph will provide valuable practice on a relatively small scale. In this book, therefore, we will examine the expository paragraph. In particular, we will study the *general-to-specific* (or *g–s*) expository paragraph—the paragraph that opens with a general statement and goes on to support that statement with appropriate examples and details. Learning to write an effective g–s paragraph means learning the skills and concepts that are essential to good writing in general. And because the g–s paragraph is, in a sense, an essay in miniature, mastering the paragraph should help you to master longer forms of writing as well.

The General-to-Specific Paragraph

Basic Structure and Purpose

The general-to-specific paragraph, like most paragraphs, is a group of sentences that work together to present a single, unified topic or idea. The first line is indented to signal the reader that a new grouping of sentences is beginning.

The length of the g–s paragraph usually ranges from about one hundred to three hundred words. This is not to say that shorter or longer paragraphs are unacceptable. Essays may even have one-sentence paragraphs, used for emphasis, and thousand-word paragraphs can provide valuable exposition in all types of writing. But we are not concerned here with very short or very long paragraphs. Rather, it is our intention to examine and construct paragraphs that are useful as practice because they are long enough to require careful development but not so long as to be unmanageable. For this purpose, the expository paragraph of about one hundred to three hundred words is the best kind to undertake.

The Importance of Specifics

The general-to-specific paragraph, as we have said, moves from a general opening statement that stands in need of support to the specifics—examples and factual details—that support the general statement. A general statement requires support, or development, if readers are to find it convincing. The details the writer furnishes enable readers to understand and evaluate the point the writer is making. For example, the following sentence is a general statement:

> *Butch Cassidy and the Sundance Kid* is one of the most entertaining movies ever made.

Unless you have particular confidence in the writer's judgment, you would need to see some evidence in support of this statement. It is up to the writer to provide you with more specific information if he or she wants to convince you that the statement is valid. In the following paragraph, written by a student, a series of specific statements supports and explains the writer's point of view:

> *Butch Cassidy and the Sundance Kid* is one of the most entertaining movies ever made. First of all, one of the biggest attractions of this movie is its co-stars, Paul Newman and Robert Redford. These two men were at or near the peaks of their careers when the movie was released, and they gave fine acting performances. In the movie, the characters they play are brave and dashing, yet somehow quite human. In addition to its marvelous stars, the movie has an exciting, adventurous plot. It follows Butch and Sundance as they rob trains and banks, elude a posse,

and go to live in Bolivia, where they continue their life of crime. At one point they even jump off a high cliff into a fast-moving river to escape pursuit. Finally, the movie depicts the life of crime—a subject that is often dealt with seriously in film—in a light and humorous way. For example, one morning, right after eluding pursuers, Butch takes time out to perform several comical feats on his new bicycle. And, of course, there is a constant flow of wit which adds levity even to grim situations.

This paragraph provides the reader with several reasons for seriously considering its opening statement. By developing that general statement, the writer has taken steps to satisfy the curiosity and skepticism it may have aroused in the reader.

Levels of Generality

An effective general-to-specific paragraph usually has at least three levels of generality. The first and most general level is the opening statement. The second level consists of more specific statements that directly support the opening statement. These, in turn, may be supported by statements that are even more specific—the third level of generality—and so on.

The following outline demonstrates how the paragraph presented above uses the general-to-specific structure:

General statement: *Butch Cassidy and the Sundance Kid* is one of the most entertaining movies ever made.

> *Specific 1:* First of all, one of the biggest attractions of this movie is its co-stars, Paul Newman and Robert Redford.
>
>> *Specific 1a:* These two men were at or near the peaks of their careers when the movie was released, and they gave fine acting performances.
>>
>> *Specific 1b:* In the movie, the characters they play are brave and dashing, yet somehow quite human.
>
> *Specific 2:* In addition to its marvelous stars, the movie has an exciting, adventurous plot.
>
>> *Specific 2a:* It follows Butch and Sundance as they rob trains and banks, elude a posse, and go to live in Bolivia, where they continue their life of crime.
>>
>> *Specific 2b:* At one point they even jump off a high cliff into a fast-moving river to escape pursuit.
>
> *Specific 3:* Finally, the movie depicts the life of crime—a subject that is often dealt with seriously in film—in a light and humorous way.
>
>> *Specific 3a:* For example, one morning, right after eluding

pursuers, Butch takes time out to perform several comical feats on his new bicycle.

Specific 3b: And, of course, there is a constant flow of wit
which adds levity even to grim situations.

As the outline indicates, the most general statement in the paragraph is the first sentence. The sentences at the next level of generality are labeled specifics 1, 2, and 3. These three sentences furnish
major points of support, but they are more convincing when pinned
down even further by the details presented in sentences 1a and 1b,
2a and 2b, and 3a and 3b. (We will discuss the movement of paragraph development through levels of supporting statements in more
depth in Chapter 3.)

Note that, because the paragraph moves from general to specific, there is no place in it for a second statement as general as
"Butch Cassidy and the Sundance Kid is one of the most entertaining movies ever made." For instance, if the sentence *"Butch Cassidy
and the Sundance Kid* can in many ways be compared with *The
Sting"* were inserted in the paragraph, the focus of the paragraph
would shift. The new statement has little to do with the content of
the rest of the paragraph, and, furthermore, it is itself broad enough
to require a whole paragraph of specific comparisons for support. It
cannot, because of its level of generality, function as support in this
paragraph.

SUMMARY

1. To understand the basics of clear writing, it is useful to examine
   first the general-to-specific (g–s) paragraph.
2. A g–s paragraph is a group of sentences, set apart from preceding material by indentation, that present a unified topic or
   idea.
3. Most g–s paragraphs are from one hundred to three hundred
   words in length.
4. The g–s paragraph moves from a general opening statement to
   specific supporting statements.
5. The g–s paragraph is usually built with three levels of generality:
   the general opening statement, less general supporting statements, and further details that elaborate on the supporting statements.
6. No other sentence of the same level of generality as the opening
   statement should appear in the paragraph.

EXERCISES

I. In this chapter you have seen that a g–s paragraph moves from a general opening statement to specific supporting statements and details. This exercise will give you practice in distinguishing the general from the specific. Examine the following sentences and decide whether each sentence, if used in a g–s paragraph, would serve as a general statement requiring further support or a specific statement requiring no further support.

    A. There are several stages of alcoholism.

    B. The general's parents moved to New York in 1843.

    C. The queen of England lives in Buckingham Palace.

    D. It is difficult to be married to a physician.

    E. Education should do more than merely teach skills.

    F. The car accident occurred on the south exit ramp of the highway.

    G. Being a member of a social club has definite advantages for a college student.

    H. Boston has a number of famous buildings that date back to the American Revolution.

II. Study the lists below carefully and rearrange the items according to the level of generality they represent. To do this, first select the item in each group that represents the most general category; then pick out the three items in each group that are in the second-most-general category; and, finally, decide which items belong in the most specific category. The first group has been completed as a model.

Model:

Mammals	*General Heading:* __Animals__
Trout	1. __Mammals__
Whales	a: __Humans__
Seagulls	b: __Bears__
Humans	c: __Whales__
Sharks	2. __Fish__
Bass	a: __Sharks__
Animals	b: __Trout__
Thrushes	c: __Bass__
Fish	3. __Birds__
Robins	a: __Seagulls__

Bears   b: *Robins*

Birds   c: *Thrushes*

A. Refrigerator
Bureau
Kitchen
Oven
Furniture
Bedroom
Couch
Coffee table
Wardrobe
Cupboard
Living room
Easy chair
Bed

B. Student union
Blackboards
Desks
Classroom building
Snacks
Lectures
Reference books
Library
Music and conversation
Study carrels
Buildings on campus
Disorderly tables and chairs

C. Gives easy exams
Gives difficult exams
Easy
Assigns a great deal of reading
Doesn't care if we attend
Has a strict attendance policy
Two types of teachers I have had
Assigns little writing
Gives lengthy writing assignments
Doesn't keep us for the full class period
Hard
Keeps us for the full class period
   and then some
Assigns very little reading

III. The following paragraphs, taken from student writing, move successfully through varying levels of generality. Read the paragraphs carefully and then indicate in the blank before each sentence its level of generality. Use *GS* (general statement) to indicate a sentence that is at the first level of generality and that the other sentences support. Use Arabic numerals (1,2,3) to indicate sentences that are at the second level of generality and lower-case letters (a,b,c) to indicate sentences that are at the third level of generality.

Model:

> *GS* Sunbathing, a popular summer pastime, is considered by many doctors to have several bad effects which sunbathers should know more about. *1* Prolonged exposure to the sun, even on mild days, may cause sunstroke, a health hazard many people choose to ignore when pursuing a tan. *2* Rashes and severe burns are another common condition among sunbathers. *2a* Although a minor sunburn can be painful, a severe sunburn is a serious illness and must be treated by a physician. *3* Dry skin, also an effect of sunbathing, can produce facial wrinkles, especially if the sunbather is more than forty years old. *4* But by far the most serious effect of excessive exposure to the sun is the risk of skin cancer. *4a* Although medical authorities have demonstrated that many forms of skin cancer are caused by the sun, thousands of Americans risk their health in their foolish desire to acquire a tan.

> **A.** _____ Several types of people come into a 7-Eleven store on a regular basis. _____ During the day, dirty-faced slurpee kids ride up on their bikes. _____ Jingling change in their pockets, they take forever to decide which flavor of slurpee they want. _____ Occasionally, upon deciding, they ask if they can have an extra dash of syrup; then, when you oblige them and hand the slurpee over to them, they run away without saying thanks. _____ And there are the pinball addicts—the older kids who hang around after school, poised with hands gripping the sides of the machine and jerking it occasionally to help the ball get into the slot. _____ The addicts and their friends, when they are not asking for change for a dollar or watching other addicts at the machine, are thumbing through the magazines that they are not legally old enough to buy. _____ For excitement in the wee hours, there is the town drunk, who staggers in with tattered clothing and an unshaven face. _____ He usually asks for a cup of coffee in a loud voice. _____ When he pays, he is always a nickel short.

B. _____ Walking has recently become extremely popular among people of all ages. _____ One important reason is the physical benefit of added strength and stamina which walking provides. _____ In their off-seasons, professional athletes often walk or hike when they are not exercising more rigorously. _____ Young people are now walking where they used to ride so that they can stay healthy and participate in physical activities. _____ A second reason for the popularity of walking is that a brisk walk can burn off calories and fat. _____ Dieters and people who have jobs that do not require a great deal of physical activity often walk because of this benefit. _____ And, finally, walking is especially popular among older people who find other forms of exercise too strenuous. _____ On the advice of a doctor, an older person can walk many blocks or even many miles a day without running the risk of a heart attack.

C. _____ In order to have a beautifully finished piece of ceramic pottery, certain steps must be followed. _____ After the piece has been removed from its mold, each seam must be sanded so that it is perfectly smooth. _____ The piece must next be washed very lightly with a wet sponge to remove any dust particles that may adhere to it. _____ The piece is then placed in a kiln and fired to the required hardness before color is applied. _____ After this first firing, the color of ceramic glaze is selected and brushed on the piece with as even a stroke as possible to prevent shade variations during firing. _____ Most colors must be applied at least three times to ensure true color. _____ If a design is desired on the piece, the design must be placed on it by tracing, gluing, or freehand drawing. _____ This process should be completed before the piece is colored. _____ Pottery with a design traced on it, however, is usually glazed with clear glaze. _____ When the color or glaze has dried completely, the piece is placed back in the kiln for a final firing.

Chapter 2

How to Begin Writing Paragraphs

For some writing assignments, you may be given a specific topic to write about or be asked to choose from among several topics. For other assignments, you may be allowed complete freedom to write on a topic of your own choosing. Either way, it is likely that you will have to decide what aspect of your topic to focus on in your paragraph. The suggestions in this chapter will help you both when you select a topic of your own and when you write on a topic chosen for you.

Selecting a Suitable Topic

If your assignment is to write a paragraph on a topic of your own choosing, you may end up spending more time selecting a suitable topic than you do actually writing the paragraph. Many students have difficulty deciding what to write about and find themselves staring at a blank page while time for completing the assignment dwindles. It is true that words and ideas do not flow from the end of a pen or from the keys of a typewriter, but words will come more easily if you approach your writing systematically and follow certain guidelines.

You must, of course, write on a topic about which you have enough information to put together a convincing paragraph. You may draw on information you have gathered from such sources as television, newspapers, magazines, movies, talks with friends, or school courses. You may also draw on your own experiences. Don't underestimate your interests and activities as a source of topics for your writing or assume that others would find them boring to read about. For example, if you work part-time in a supermarket, you may be able to write a more interesting paragraph on how to pack a grocery bag than on a complex subject like inflation, foreign policy, or the morality of abortion.

The following paragraph is on a topic with which the student writer had little familiarity but which he chose because he thought it would be "interesting to the reader":

> Mexico is a land of extremes. A friend told me that during the day temperatures get very high, but at night you have to wear a coat. The streets of cities like Acapulco are crowded with square stone haciendas, green trees, and gorgeous flowers; but these cities contrast sharply with Mexico's deserts, which are populated only by lizards and cactus plants. A television commercial once showed someone diving from one of the high cliffs near Acapulco. These cliffs are spectacular. The Aztecs who used to dive from these cliffs had developed an advanced civilization. They knew a great deal about building and about astronomy. In fact, they had cities and temples and art long before the United States was ever thought of.

Obviously the writer had never been to Mexico and had not acquired enough knowledge of his topic to provide support for his opening sentence. What he knows about Mexico as a "land of extremes" is exhausted after a few sentences, so he fills out the paragraph with sketchy bits of information, drifting from a discussion of a modern diver, to Aztec divers, to Aztec civilization. None of this information provides specifics that support his description of Mexico as a "land of extremes."

The next paragraph, on a topic about which the student writer clearly had first-hand experience, is more satisfactory:

> Taking a test is a nerve-racking experience for me. Even if I have done well in homework assignments and have studied hard, when the test questions are handed out, my hands become sweaty, my heart begins to pound, and my hands shake so much I can hardly hold my pencil. All during the test, I am afraid that I am failing it. Even the simplest questions become very difficult for me. If anyone coughs, my attention is instantly drawn to him. The time seems to pass too quickly. Each time the instructor announces the time remaining for completion of the test, I become more nervous. When the instructor says that we have only a few minutes to finish, I panic even if I have already finished and am going back to check my answers.

The writer has given us valid reasons to accept his general opening statement. The more specific statements that follow the opening statement convince us that taking a test is, for him, an ordeal.

The following is a successful paragraph which contains information derived from reading rather than from personal experience. The student writer satisfied her curiosity about Mexico by taking some time to read about it in the library. From her research, she gained enough information on the topic she chose, "Mexican foods," to write a successful general-to-specific paragraph. Her opening statement is followed by specifics that develop her general idea:

> Some of the principal foods of Mexico have come down from the days of the Aztecs. For example, corn was the basic item in Aztec cooking, and it is still basic today. Tortillas made from corn flour are among the most popular foods in Mexico and are a staple of the Mexican diet. In addition, tamales are steamed in corn husks according to the same process used in ancient Mexico. There is also a corn soup called *pozole,* which has retained its popularity among the people of Mexico for centuries. The same kinds of fowl which graced Aztec tables hundreds of years ago please Mexican palates today, and many of the fruits which were plentiful in Aztec times are still found in Mexican markets.

Topic Ideas

If you are asked to write on a topic of your own choosing and have trouble thinking of one, you may find consideration of the following list of broad subject areas helpful:

adult education	dormitory life	movies
advertisements	drug abuse	music
anxiety	enemies	pets
automobiles	exercise	politics
camping	fears	recreation
clothes	gardening	sex
dancing	hairstyles	slogans
dating	hobbies	sports
depression	holidays	status symbols
diets	hunting	study habits
discrimination	innocence	television
diseases	jobs	

These subject areas may suggest more specific topics on which you could write an effective paragraph. Each of the following topics, for example, is derived from a subject on the list and might be suitable for the type of writing you will be doing:

courses in home repair (adult education)
going to the dentist (anxiety)
how to pick a used car (automobiles)
dancing school (dancing)
television dating programs (dating)

when to break a diet (diets)
women and job promotions (discrimination)
dormitory laundry facilities (dormitory life)
campus drug users (drug abuse)
a hobby I could never get into (hobbies)
losing one's innocence (innocence)
movies on Sunday afternoon (movies)
"Nobody can do it like———can." (slogans)

EXERCISE

Using the list of thirty-five broad subject areas, make a list of ten specific topics, other than those in the list above, on which you might write a paragraph. Remember that a good topic is one that you know enough about, through personal experience or through reading, to write a convincing paragraph on.

The Topic Sentence and the Controlling Idea

Whether you select a topic yourself or are assigned one by your instructor, once you have a topic you are ready to think about constructing a paragraph. In the general-to-specific paragraph, the first sentence announces your topic and makes a general statement about it that the rest of the paragraph will explain or justify. This sentence is known as the *topic sentence.* The remaining sentences in the paragraph are subordinate to it and, as we have seen, provide specific supporting ideas. Because the entire paragraph is constructed around the topic sentence, this sentence is the most important one in the paragraph.

Not only does the topic sentence announce what the paragraph is about, but, even more important, it also conveys the *controlling idea.* To understand this concept, consider the second paragraph on Mexico (p. 11). It is clear from the opening sentence that the topic of the paragraph is "Mexican foods." But besides identifying the topic, the topic sentence signals to the reader what *aspect* of the topic the writer will focus on. Here we learn that the author will show that many modern Mexican foods *have come down from the days of the Aztecs.* This idea—the aspect of the topic that will be focused on in the paragraph—is the controlling idea. As in this example, the controlling idea is expressed in certain words or phrases that appear in the topic sentence.

Understanding the difference between a topic and a controlling idea, both of which are essential to the topic sentence, is an important step toward writing successful paragraphs. A topic alone cannot give your paragraph the needed focus and direction. For example, look at the following items:

1. The energy shortage
2. The energy shortage will have several beneficial effects on the American people.
3. There are many ways to beat the energy shortage.
4. The energy shortage is responsible for some changes in American life.

Item 1 is simply a topic. By itself it does not suggest any one aspect of the energy shortage for the writer to focus on. But item 1 can be more narrowly focused in several ways; items 2, 3, and 4 suggest three possibilities. Item 2 can be used as a topic sentence, conveying the controlling idea that the energy shortage will have beneficial effects on Americans. The sentence communicates both the topic of the paragraph—"the energy shortage"—and the focus of the paragraph, signaled by the words *beneficial effects on the American people.* Item 3 is also suitable for use as a topic sentence. Here, the topic is stated at the end of the sentence, and the words signaling the focus are *many ways to beat.* In item 4, the topic is again at the beginning of the sentence, and the words indicating the focus are *changes in American life.* Unlike 1, either 2, 3, or 4 can be used as a topic sentence expressing a controlling idea, and any one of the three, when so used, will provide a good beginning for a general-to-specific paragraph.

EXERCISES

I. In each of the following sentences, identify (1) the *topic* and (2) the controlling idea—the special words or phrases that state the aspect of the topic the writers will focus on.

Model:

> Freshman English is a time-consuming course.
> *Topic:* Freshman English
> *Focusing word:* time-consuming

A. A woman who works full-time and also runs a household has busy evenings.
B. A good wine is easily identified by three traits.
C. Drop/add policies at this school are too lenient.

D. Planting a garden yields many rewards.

E. College registration can be a frustrating experience.

F. Severe winters create several problems for the conscientious energy consumer.

G. The crusade to save the great whales from extinction is a crucial ecological last stand.

H. To annoy the viewer seems to be the only purpose behind some television commercials.

I. *Flamboyant* is the word to describe many of today's fashions.

J. Self-deprecation has been the bread and butter of such successful comedians as Woody Allen, Johnny Carson, and Joan Rivers.

II. For each of the following topics, construct a good topic sentence that expresses a controlling idea.

Model:

> *Topic:* cooking
> *Topic sentence:* Cooking today involves the use of many time-saving devices.

A. designing a living room

B. a recent campus election

C. television talk shows

D. dieting

E. coed dormitories

F. cycling

G. "Doonesbury" (or any other comic strip)

H. being a secretary

Deciding on a Controlling Idea

Because the controlling idea is crucial to the success of a paragraph, don't start to write a paragraph until you have decided on *both* your topic and your controlling idea. If you simply start writing about a topic with no controlling idea in mind, you may wander off in different directions and deal with a number of ideas, each of which could be better developed in a separate paragraph.

Potential for Development

The controlling idea expressed in the topic sentence of an expository paragraph must, of course, require development; otherwise, you would have no reason for writing. Consider, for example, this sentence:

John was born in Chicago.

Such a sentence would not be a good topic sentence for a g–s paragraph because it would be difficult to develop; it is a statement of fact which does not need explanation or expansion. Consider, on the other hand, the following sentence:

The fact that John was born in Chicago had a profound effect on his life.

This sentence can be used as a topic sentence because it expresses an idea that can be developed in the paragraph: you would go on to explain how being born in Chicago affected John's life.

One mark of a workable controlling idea—here, that John's being born in Chicago affected his life profoundly—is that it raises a question or a series of questions that you, as the writer, are expected to discuss in your paragraph. In this case, the questions raised might include the following: Was John's career determined by the place of his birth? Did Chicago shape his character? Did it affect his health? Were his family life and education in any way influenced by the city? Answering such questions is your responsibility, and the skill with which you answer them will determine the effectiveness of your writing.

At the same time, you should avoid using a topic sentence with a controlling idea that is too vague for effective discussion. For example:

Colorado is a great place.

This sentence is just as difficult to develop as the topic sentence "John was born in Chicago," but for a different reason. The "Chicago" sentence provides no controlling idea to develop into a g–s paragraph; the "Colorado" sentence, because its idea is not narrow enough, fails to indicate a particular direction for development.

The strengths of the topic sentence "Some of the principal foods of Mexico have come down from the days of the Aztecs" are not only that it announces the topic and commits the writer to developing it but also that it requires the writer to discuss *nothing but* the similarities in diet and cooking between present-day Mexicans and the ancient Aztecs. Having settled on this particular topic sentence, the writer could not go on to compare Mexican foods and American foods, nor could she consider the cost of food to the consumer today.

The Topic Sentence as Contract

You may find it helpful to think of a topic sentence as a *contract*. In effect, with the choice of a topic and a controlling idea and the expression of both in the topic sentence, writers establish a contract between themselves and their readers. The responsibility of the writer is to convince the reader that the topic sentence is believable. The degree to which the writer succeeds in fulfilling the terms of the contract determines how effective the paragraph will be.

Again, look at the paragraph on Mexican foods (p. 11). The writer's topic sentence, "Some of the principal foods of Mexico have come down from the days of the Aztecs," establishes a definite contract. The remaining sentences in the paragraph must support the idea that the people of Mexico are still eating foods which the ancient Aztecs ate and thus carry out the contract established between the writer and the reader in the topic sentence. The writer of the paragraph on p. 10, whose topic sentence is "Mexico is a land of extremes," also establishes a contract. But instead of supporting his idea by demonstrating the extremes to be found in Mexico, he wanders off to other subjects, so that by the end of the paragraph the reader has little evidence that Mexico indeed is "a land of extremes." The paragraph is unsuccessful because the writer has not fulfilled his contract.

SUMMARY

1. The writer's first concern is to find an appropriate topic on which to write a paragraph.
2. The writer should be familiar enough with the topic, either through experience or research, to develop it effectively in the paragraph.
3. The topic sentence is the first sentence in a general-to-specific paragraph and expresses the topic and the controlling idea of the paragraph. The rest of the paragraph explains or justifies the topic sentence.
4. The controlling idea limits the topic by focusing on one aspect of it and thus determines the direction that the rest of the paragraph will take. The aspect to be focused on is signaled by certain significant words or phrases in the topic sentence.
5. The topic sentence establishes a contract between the writer and the reader. The writer's obligation is to fulfill that contract by developing clearly the aspect of the topic which is expressed by the controlling idea.

EXERCISES

I. Supply topic sentences for the following paragraphs. Be certain that each topic sentence conveys a clear controlling idea.

Model:

Successfully transplanting a tree requires careful attention to details.

Before planting, check to see if the tree's roots are moist; if they are not, soak them in water for two or more hours until they appear soggy. While the roots are soaking, find a sunny spot in which to plant the tree. The soil should be a dark brown color —indicating that it is rich in nutrients. If the soil is in poor condition, mix in peat moss or potting soil. Next, dig a hole big enough to allow the tree's roots room to spread out. Place the tree in the hole and, while holding the tree straight, fill in the hole with dirt; pack the dirt lightly. Water the tree every day for a week so that the roots can take hold in the ground.

A. _____

Home computers can perform tedious bookkeeping tasks that most families never seem to have time to do properly. They can balance checkbooks in seconds, endearing themselves immediately to those of us who are always overdrawing our accounts. They can easily keep track of family budgets and aid in the filling out of income tax forms. In addition, home computers can provide entertainment for the whole family. There are, of course, many computer games on the market that can be enjoyed by children and adults. And with a little study of programming techniques, buyers can learn to program their own games. There are many other applications for home computers as well. Computers can be programmed to control heating systems, to function as security systems, or to act as an efficient memo pad for important messages and dates.

B. _____

Swollen rivers and streams have risen over their banks, flooding almost every field in the area. Those fields that have somehow escaped flooding are for the most part unworkable, even with today's modern equipment. Cattle are stranded in isolated areas without food and will remain so until the water recedes and the farm owners can bring them relief. Because hay that normally would have been baled will probably rot in the fields, farmers will have to buy more expensive feeds. Although the forecast calls for the rain to end tonight, farmers will undoubtedly feel the effects of today's downpour for many weeks to come.

C._____

Documentaries, particularly those that deal with aspects of nature, are often shown on television. "The Undersea World of Jacques Cousteau" and the "National Geographic Specials" fit into this category. Dramas derived from events in history, such as *Roots* and *Holocaust,* are becoming increasingly popular. Programs like these familiarize viewers with real situations and raise important questions concerning the outcome and lasting effects of historical events. While ballets, operas, concerts, and plays appear infrequently on commercial television, they are often aired on educational networks. Specifically, several national acting companies, the Metropolitan Opera, the New York Philharmonic, and even the Bolshoi ballet can, at the flick of a switch, entertain viewers in their living rooms. Finally, television for children has made great advances, moving away from the Saturday morning cartoons and toward such educationally oriented programs as "Sesame Street," "Zoom," and "The Electric Company."

II. Write a paragraph for one of the following topic sentences. Feel free to alter the topic sentence according to your preferences, opinions, and experiences. For example, if you have never thought of buying a home but are an avid automobile enthusiast, you might alter sentence D to read, "An automobile is a worthwhile investment."

   A. Commuting to school has its advantages and its disadvantages.

   B. Taking birth control pills can be risky.

   C. A habitually slow driver is as dangerous as a speedster.

   D. A home is a good investment.

   E. Final exams should be abolished.

   F. Quiet people make better friends than do talkative people.

   G. Instructors who grade leniently are not always the best teachers.

Chapter 3

Paragraph Unity
and Structure

In Chapters 1 and 2 you learned what a general-to-specific paragraph is and how to begin writing one. In this chapter you will learn how to put a paragraph together so that it will be unified. You will recall from Chapter 2 that the general-to-specific paragraph begins with a topic sentence which establishes the *topic* and conveys a *controlling idea,* the idea that is to be developed in the paragraph. The statement of the controlling idea in the topic sentence focuses the paragraph on one aspect of the topic.

What Is Paragraph Unity?

As you learned in Chapter 2, the topic sentence has a special relationship to the other sentences in the paragraph. It is a contract that you as writer establish with your reader. To fulfill the contract and satisfy the reader that your topic sentence is valid, you must see to it that every sentence in the paragraph supports the controlling idea expressed in the topic sentence. If any does not, your paragraph will not be unified and will not communicate effectively. On the other hand, if every sentence in the paragraph provides direct or indirect support for the controlling idea, your paragraph will be unified. Every expository paragraph, no matter how short or how long, must be unified to be effective.

An important point must be made here: not all sentences that relate in some way to the *topic* of a paragraph *necessarily* help to unify the paragraph. A sentence may be related to the topic of the paragraph and provide information that is accurate and interesting,

19

but a sentence that doesn't support the *controlling idea* of the paragraph will destroy the paragraph's unity.

To understand the importance of unity, examine the following paragraph, which is *not* unified:

(1) Pilots are the primary cause of many aircraft accidents. (2) Ignoring their responsibilities, many pilots fail to perform their duties efficiently, and tragedy has too often been the needless result. (3) History records that many fatal accidents have occurred, for example, because pilots failed to listen to the advice of air traffic controllers who were in a position to warn them about impending disasters. (4) To become an air traffic controller, one must be extremely intelligent. (5) Sometimes pilots are overtired, and they neglect to take the precautions necessary to avoid accidents. (6) They may even be taking drugs which slow down their physical reactions. (7) As we all know, statistics have proved that the number of college students who abuse drugs is increasing at an alarming rate, and few of these students realize that if they continue to use drugs they will never be able to enter a career in aviation. (8) Sometimes accidents occur through a malfunction in the plane's equipment. (9) A door may open during flight, or a tire may blow out as the plane takes off. (10) Pilots, of course, aren't responsible for accidents such as these. (11) Perhaps most startling is the fact that every year one or two air traffic accidents are caused by student pilots who attempt journeys beyond their capabilities and end up producing catastrophes which destroy life and property. (12) Because they don't employ student pilots, commercial airlines are the safest form of air transportation. (13) The next time you take a commercial flight, you should be sure to ask yourself the following questions: Does the pilot look happy and healthy? Does the plane seem sound and sturdy? What are the weather conditions outside?

You probably had difficulty following the writer's reasoning in this paragraph. While all of the sentences in the paragraph relate at least in some way to the *topic,* "aircraft accidents," the paragraph is not unified because not every sentence supports the *controlling idea* that *"pilots are the primary cause* of many aircraft accidents."

If we look at each of the sentences in this paragraph individually, we find that the following sentences do not belong because they do not lend support to the controlling idea:

(4) To become an air traffic controller, one must be extremely intelligent.

(7) As we all know, statistics have proved that the number of college students who abuse drugs is increasing at an alarming rate, and few

of these students realize that if they continue to use drugs they will never be able to enter a career in aviation.

(8) Sometimes accidents occur through a malfunction in the plane's equipment.

(9) A door may open during flight, or a tire may blow out as the plane takes off.

(10) Pilots, of course, aren't responsible for accidents such as these.

(12) Because they don't employ student pilots, commercial airlines are the safest form of air transportation.

(13) The next time you take a commercial flight, you should be sure to ask yourself the following questions: Does the pilot look happy and healthy? Does the plane seem sound and sturdy? What are the weather conditions outside?

In these sentences the writer discusses qualifications for air traffic controllers, drug abuse among students who might wish to become pilots, mechanical malfunctions, and commercial airline safety; he even provides a list of precautionary questions for the commercial airline passenger. But since none of these sentences supports the controlling idea that *"pilots are the primary cause* of many aircraft accidents," they detract from the unity of the paragraph. With each sentence we wonder what the writer is saying and why; we may even stop reading as we lose track of the idea we thought we were following.

The other sentences in the paragraph do support the controlling idea. If the writer had included only those sentences, the result would have been a more compact and unified paragraph, as we can see by reading through the list below:

(1) Pilots are the primary cause of many aircraft accidents. (topic sentence)

(2) Ignoring their responsibilities, many pilots fail to perform their duties efficiently, and tragedy has too often been the needless result.

(3) History records that many fatal accidents have occurred, for example, because pilots failed to listen to the advice of air traffic controllers who were in a position to warn them about impending disasters.

(5) Sometimes pilots are overtired, and they neglect to take the precautions necessary to avoid accidents.

(6) They may even be taking drugs which slow down their physical reactions.

(11) Perhaps most startling is the fact that every year one or two air traffic accidents are caused by student pilots who attempt journeys beyond their capabilities and end up producing catastrophes which destroy life and property.

SUMMARY

1. Every expository paragraph, no matter how short or how long, must be unified.

2. In a unified general-to-specific paragraph, every sentence supports the controlling idea, expressed in the paragraph's topic sentence.

3. In general, the more unified a paragraph is, the clearer and more convincing it will be.

EXERCISES

I. Read each of the following paragraphs carefully. Specify the controlling idea expressed in the topic sentence and then examine the paragraph for unity. Identify by number any sentence that does not support the paragraph's controlling idea.

   A. (1) Two methods that horse owners use to make their horses fit for riding are "gentle breaking" and "bronco busting." (2) To "gentle break" a horse means simply to train it, through coaxing and reward, to submit willingly to its owner's commands. (3) Horses trained through the gentle-breaking method usually retain their free spirit but allow themselves to be handled and ridden by their owners because of the mutual trust which develops between the rider and the animal. (4) The "gentling" technique, as it is also called, was learned from the Plains Indians, who needed well-trained and obedient horses. (5) As we all know, the Plains Indians lived in the West, so they depended on horses for transportation. (6) Sitting Bull was a Plains Indian. (7) He fought at Wounded Knee, possibly on a horse which had been trained through the gentle-breaking method. (8) In the bronco-busting method, on the other hand, the rider forces the horse into submission by attempting to stay mounted on the animal until it stops bucking, running, or rearing. (9) The bronco-busting method also originated in the Old West and is most often seen today in rodeo games. (10) Because the bronco method is more forceful than the gentle method, horses trained by it are usually less spirited and more submissive than are horses which undergo the gentle treatment.

   B. (1) Air pollution has several damaging effects on the environment. (2) It soils clothes and may even rot them. (3) Flowers, shrubs, and trees don't grow well in places where there is too much air pollution. (4) In addition, dirty air sickens farm animals and has been known to damage food crops. (5) Further, it rusts metal and disfigures historic monuments and public buildings. (6) Some of the statues, for example, on Notre Dame Cathedral in France have begun to deteriorate as a result of prolonged exposure to polluted air. (7) Notre Dame was built during the Middle Ages and is one of France's most historic landmarks. (8) Air pollution also destroys the landscape beauty this earth abounds in by hiding it behind a haze of filth. (9) Finally, extended exposure to air pollution can also affect vision and breathing in humans. (10) Even mild doses of air pollution have been known to bring on heart attacks and lung disorders.

C. (1) A successful rummage sale requires advance preparation. (2) Approximately two weeks before the sale, a location should be selected. (3) The location should be easy for people to find and large enough to accommodate anticipated crowds and provide display areas for the items for sale. (4) For the rummage sale to be a success, moreover, advance advertising is essential. (5) Local and regional papers and magazines should carry ads about the sale. (6) Well in advance of the day of the sale, signs should be made that will direct prospective buyers to the sale. (7) Posters announcing the sale should be displayed in churches, stores, and other public places. (8) During the week preceding the sale, the merchandise to be sold should be categorized and priced. (9) Clothing, for example, should be separated from appliances and tools. (10) Most clothing purchased at rummage sales is a good buy. (11) Many people come just to get a bargain on the price of clothes. (12) Finally, change should be obtained from the bank. (13) Because most purchases range from five to seventy-five cents, a plentiful supply of nickels, dimes, and quarters is a necessity at a rummage sale.

D. (1) The living conditions in many city jails are appalling. (2) Many of the jail cells aren't fit for human habitation. (3) They are often filthy and unsanitary. (4) Disinfectant and cleaning agents are rarely used. (5) Roaches and rats scuttle across the floors looking for crumbs of food. (6) Roaches, of course, are difficult to get rid of even in clean places. (7) Scientists say that roaches have changed little since prehistoric times and that if the world were to experience an atomic holocaust, roaches would be one of the few living creatures to survive. (8) In addition, many city jails are overcrowded. (9) As many as three or four inmates sleep in cells which are only twelve feet wide and twelve feet long. (10) Finally, because the pay is limited, there aren't always enough guards in the jails. (11) When violence arises, guards, fearing for their own safety, are afraid to take proper action. (12) In some city jails, murders and suicides have occurred because guards were occupied in other parts of the building and were unable to arrive in time to prevent them.

E. (1) Since the beginning of time, hunting has been a part of human life. (2) Early man had to hunt to provide food for himself and his family. (3) Hunting also supplied him with clothing, tools, oils, and jewelry. (4) During the Middle Ages hunting served as entertainment and sport, as well as a means of getting food. (5) Some of the characters in Chaucer's *Canterbury Tales* hunted. (6) Today hunting still has its attractions. (7) Clubs give trophies to people who are skilled hunters. (8) Most hunters own dogs. (9) Training a hunting dog properly requires special patience and skill. (10) Did you know that the dog which won the A.C.H.A. World Hunt in 1977 is now worth $2,700? (11) No wonder dogs are man's best friends!

Planning and Constructing a Unified. Paragraph

We have seen that paragraph unity can sometimes be improved simply by eliminating from completed paragraphs those sentences that don't support the controlling idea. However, you cannot rely on this method alone to achieve paragraph unity. Writers generally agree that *the best way to achieve unity is to plan your work carefully.* Once you have written a topic sentence, you face the task of organizing the body of your paragraph so that it convincingly supports your controlling idea. To do this within the limited framework of a one-hundred- to three-hundred-word paragraph requires discipline and thought. You must judiciously select your supporting evidence and clearly relate all the sentences in the paragraph to your controlling idea.

Preliminary Steps

You will find it easier to write effective paragraphs if you develop your ideas systematically. Begin this process with the following important steps:

1. *Select a topic and a controlling idea and write a topic sentence in which they are expressed.* This step was discussed in Chapter 2.

2. *Jot down the facts and ideas which you think will support your controlling idea.* For this initial list, you may simply write down a word or a phrase for each thought that comes to mind. Don't hesitate to include all or most of what occurs to you; at this point you are simply accumulating material which you will sort through and examine at a later stage. You are by no means committed to using any particular fact or idea in the final paragraph.

3. *Rewrite each fact or idea in the form of a complete sentence.* These sentences are preliminary and need not be elaborate or polished. By converting each fact or idea to sentence form, you can better evaluate its usefulness.

4. *Read back over your list of preliminary sentences and ask yourself whether your controlling idea is valid.* You need not examine each item in your list closely at this point. Simply scan the list to get a sense of whether or not you have enough supporting material to develop your controlling idea convincingly. If you are uncertain, you need to reexamine your topic sentence. You may have selected a controlling idea that simply isn't true and can't be supported or that is either too broad or too specific for sensible development (see pages 14–15). On the other hand, it may be that you don't know enough about your topic to support your controlling idea and that you need to learn more, either by searching through your own experiences or by doing further research. If you find that you have problems with your controlling idea, *now* is the time to catch and correct them. You cannot write an effective paragraph if your controlling idea is difficult to support.

Let's consider how this process works. Suppose that your topic is "Tutankhamen's tomb" and that you have decided on the controlling idea expressed in the following topic sentence:

> When the British archeologist Howard Carter excavated the tomb of the Pharoah Tutankhamen, he discovered an astonishing treasure of ancient Egyptian artwork.

The controlling idea in this sentence is signalled by the phrase *an astonishing treasure of ancient Egyptian artwork.*

The next step is to jot down a list of facts and ideas which you think will support your topic sentence. Your preliminary list might look like this:

> Tut's four coffins: one within another; several thousand pounds
> antechamber: filled with furniture, statues and carvings, and chests of beautiful objects

antechamber: golden throne in center, with arms in the form of winged
    serpents
antechamber: intricately carved alabaster vessels near throne, and two
    life-size varnished black statues, probably of the king
shrines: surrounded by fans, oars, etc. on floor—for afterlife
jars and chests (for food and drink) in treasury
mummy wrapped in scented linens—exotic perfumes (aroma lasted!)
belief in afterlife—careful preparation of tomb for afterlife
gold burial mask on mummy
mask: inlaid with semiprecious stones and glass paste—dazzling
two small coffins (deceased children)
jars (Tut's embalmed entrails)
alabaster vessel at entrance
mask: perfect likeness of Tut
magnificent murals on walls, brightly painted (yellow, red, black, white)
wall paintings show king's afterlife
one wall: baboon spirits of funerary realm through which dead king
    would pass
mummy: jewels found in shroud
antechamber: alabaster lamp

Now go back and put each note into sentence form. The result
is a list of statements to consider as possible support for your topic
sentence.

(a) Tut's four coffins, one within the other, weighed several thousand
pounds.

(b) The antechamber of the tomb was filled with furniture, statues and
carvings, and chests containing beautiful objects.

(c) In the center of the antechamber was a golden throne with arms
in the form of winged serpents.

(d) Near the throne were intricately carved alabaster vessels and life-
size black varnished statues, probably portraying Tutankhamen.

(e) On the floor around the shrines were fans, oars, and other items for
the afterlife.

(f) Jars and chests that contained food and drink were stashed in the
treasury.

(g) The mummy was wrapped in linen scented with exotic perfumes
whose fragrance had lasted through the centuries.

(h) Most Egyptians believed in an afterlife, and they prepared their
tombs carefully.

(i) On the mummy was found a gold burial mask.

(j) The dazzling mask was inlaid with semiprecious stones and glass
paste.

(k) Jars contained the embalmed entrails of Tut, and small coffins held
the remains of two children.

(l) A vessel of alabaster stood in the entrance to the tomb.

(m) The gold burial mask was a perfect likeness of Tut.

(n) On the walls of the tomb were a number of magnificent murals, brightly painted in red, yellow, black, and white.

(o) The wall paintings depicted events in the king's afterlife.

(p) One wall showed the baboon spirits of the funerary realm through which the dead king would pass.

(q) Many jewels were found in the shrouds of the mummy.

(r) An alabaster lamp was in the antechamber.

Once you have listed the facts and ideas to use as support for your controlling idea and have converted each item into sentence form, you are ready to begin selecting from the list what you need to develop a carefully structured paragraph. But before you proceed, take one moment to evaluate your controlling idea in light of the facts and ideas you have accumulated. Is your controlling idea valid? You answer this question by scanning your list of sentences to see whether you have enough supporting material to develop your controlling idea convincingly. Looking back over the sentences that have been listed as possible support for the controlling idea that archeologist Howard Carter discovered *an astonishing treasure of ancient Egyptian artwork* in King Tut's tomb, you can see that there are many such treasures mentioned: the throne, the statues, the burial mask, the paintings, and more. Thus, you can proceed to the next stage of organizing your paragraph with a reasonable amount of assurance that you can support your controlling idea convincingly.

Primary Supports

Once you have completed the four preliminary steps, you are ready to begin putting the pieces of your paragraph together. Your first task is to reexamine your list of sentences carefully and to identify those sentences that provide *direct* support for your controlling idea. Such sentences are called *primary supports.*

Keep the following two guidelines in mind as you choose primary supports for your paragraph. First, you should limit your selection to items which are *most likely* to convince your reader of the validity of your controlling idea. Second, you should choose sentences that can function appropriately at the second level of generality in your paragraph (as was discussed on pages 3–4 of Chapter 1). This means that, on the one hand, a primary support should be less general than the topic sentence (the first level of generality) and should provide details that directly support the topic sentence. And, on the other hand, a primary support should itself be a sentence that, if necessary, can be further developed and supported by sentences at a third level of generality.

In selecting primary supports, always remember that your goal is to support the controlling idea expressed in the topic sentence. When you sort through the sentences you have listed as possible supporting statements, analyze each to see how much support it would actually contribute to the controlling idea. Some sentences may relate to your topic but have little or no connection with your controlling idea. Other sentences may relate to your controlling idea yet not help to prove it convincingly if you are unable to develop them further or if, in your judgment, they are simply not significant. Still other sentences may contain details that you wish to use at the third level of generality—that is, in support of sentences of primary support. And finally, some sentences may be too general to be used in the context of this particular paragraph.

In the initial stages of planning the paragraph on Tutankhamen, for example, you would find that most of your sentences have to be set aside for one or another of these reasons. Sentence **a** (about Tut's coffins), sentences **e** and **f** (about everyday objects found in the tomb), sentence **g** (about the king's mummy), and sentence **k** (about small coffins and jars) relate to the topic but do little to support the controlling idea because the objects they describe are not examples of "astonishing treasures of ancient Egyptian *artwork.*" Sentences **l** (about the vessel of alabaster), **q** (about the jewels in the shrouds of the mummy), and **r** (about the alabaster lamp) may indeed describe ancient Egyptian artwork, but they could not be used very convincingly in your paragraph because you do not have enough information to develop them further. Sentences **c, d, j, m, o,** and **p** all contain specifics that could further develop a more general point expressed in another sentence. Sentence **c**, for instance, contains specifics that further develop the scene in the antechamber (introduced by sentence **b**). Sentence **h**, on the other hand, seems too general to be used as support for the paragraph's controlling idea.

Three sentences, however, stand out as suitable primary supports for the assertion that Tutankhamen's tomb contained "an astonishing treasure of ancient Egyptian artwork":

(b) The antechamber of the tomb was filled with ancient furniture, statues and carvings, and trunks containing beautiful objects.

(i) On the mummy was found a gold burial mask.

(h) On the walls of the tomb were a number of magnificent murals, brightly painted in red, yellow, black, and white.

These sentences directly and convincingly support the controlling idea of the paragraph and should provide a solid structural foundation for the finished paragraph. In the meantime, hold on to all of your other preliminary sentences. You will probably be able to use some of them to develop your primary supports when you undertake the next step in structuring your paragraph.

SUMMARY

1. The best way to achieve unity in your paragraph is through careful planning.
2. The first step in the planning process is to select a topic and a controlling idea and to write a topic sentence in which they are expressed.
3. Under your topic sentence, jot down facts and ideas which come to mind as possible support for your controlling idea.
4. Then convert the facts and ideas you have jotted down into a list of preliminary sentences.
5. Before going on, scan your list and make sure that your controlling idea is valid and supportable.
6. The next step in the planning process is to select those sentences which will best serve as primary supports for the controlling idea. Primary supports are sentences that directly support the controlling idea and that can be further developed by other details that you have listed. Primary supports constitute the second level of generality in a paragraph, as discussed in Chapter 1.

EXERCISES

I. Indicate each sentence which might serve as a primary support for the given topic sentences. Remember that primary supports must relate directly to the controlling idea and offer convincing evidence that the controlling idea is valid.

    A. *Topic Sentence:* When smokers give up their habit, they are likely to undergo a typical pattern of experiences.
      1. On the first day after they stop smoking, their enthusiasm is at a high pitch.
      2. The next few days are generally uncomfortable.
      3. Smoking is a very difficult habit to break.
      4. Part of the discomfort that they experience results from the body's elimination of various chemicals.
      5. People who quit smoking are less likely to develop lung cancer than are people who continue to smoke.
      6. After two or three weeks, the craving for tobacco gradu-

ally disappears, though it may return if the former smoker attends a social gathering where others are smoking.

7. As the craving for tobacco decreases, appetite begins to increase.

8. Even though the smoking habit is weakened, it is never broken.

9. One cigarette or one cigar can return the backslider to the ranks of confirmed smokers.

B. *Topic Sentence:* Women who drink alcohol during pregnancy risk harming their unborn children.

1. Babies born of alcoholic mothers are frequently retarded.

2. Pregnant women who drink often don't exercise as much as they should.

3. Doctors have compiled detailed studies on pregnant women who are heavy drinkers.

4. Studies have indicated that if a pregnant woman consumes an average of one or two ounces of alcohol per day, there is one chance in five that her baby will develop a serious disease called fetal alcohol syndrome.

5. Alcohol makes pregnant women feel sluggish.

6. Pregnancy often involves some degree of risk.

7. Pregnant women who are alcoholics frequently neglect their health and rarely maintain a proper diet.

8. Alcoholic women who are expecting a baby can easily forget important appointments with their physicians.

C. *Topic Sentence:* Night classes can prove extremely difficult for an eighteen-year-old college freshman.

1. Competition is more intense than in daytime courses.

2. For students who commute, getting to and from the campus is often more difficult at night than during the day.

3. Typical eighteen-year-old freshmen who live on campus prefer to spend evenings in the dormitory with their friends.

4. Night classes are often geared to the needs of older students.

5. Attending class at night often requires students to change their study habits.

6. Night classes are frequently quite tiring.

7. Ninety percent of the students in night classes are much older than the average college freshman, who often feels intimidated to the point at which he is unable to learn.

8. No one likes to finish school at ten o'clock in the evening.
9. Many of the best television programs are broadcast during the times when night classes are offered.

D. *Topic Sentence:* The electoral college is an outdated, unrepresentative, and inefficient way of electing the president of the United States.

1. Most Americans don't really understand how the electoral college works.
2. The reasons for the electoral college's coming into being are no longer important concerns.
3. Two states with unequal populations may cast the same number of popular votes, but the state with the greater population will receive more electoral votes.
4. The voters of each state do not get fair representation in the electoral college.
5. The electoral college votes do not always reflect the desires of the voting public.
6. Even though he had more popular votes, Grover Cleveland lost the 1888 presidential election to Benjamin Harrison, who had more electoral votes.
7. In some states delegates to the college aren't bound to vote for the candidates who receive the majority of their state's popular votes.
8. Eighty-one percent of the population disapprove of the electoral college.
9. No other country in the world has an electoral college.
10. Delegates to the electoral college have too much power.

II. Supply three sentences of primary support for three of the following topic sentences. Be certain that each of your primary supports relates to the controlling idea expressed in the topic sentence and not just to the topic.

Model:

Topic Sentence: Working students have special problems.
Primary Support: Their time in the library is limited.
Primary Support: Fewer courses are offered in the evenings.
Primary Support: Work often causes them to miss class.
A. *Topic Sentence:* Tragedies bring people together.

    B. *Topic Sentence:* Christmas has changed from an occasion for giving to an occasion for receiving.

    C. *Topic Sentence:* Contrary to popular opinion, blondes don't necessarily have more fun.

    D. *Topic Sentence:* Students who pay their own way through college value their education more than students who do not have to pay their own way.

    E. *Topic Sentence:* The Equal Rights Amendment would extend the rights of all minorities, as well as the rights of women.

    F. *Topic Sentence:* Many television commercials are an insult to human intelligence.

    G. *Topic Sentence:* If inflation continues to rise at an exorbitant rate, college students will no longer be able to afford the expense of dating.

Secondary Supports

Primary supports, particularly those that provide support for unfamiliar or complex controlling ideas, generally require additional information or explanation if the reader is to accept them. To supply this additional information requires additional sentences, called *secondary supports.* These sentences constitute the third level of generality discussed in Chapter 1. Instead of reinforcing the controlling idea directly, secondary supports reinforce a point or points made in a primary support. By adding information which helps make a primary support believable to the reader, they *indirectly* support the paragraph's controlling idea.

We can examine the primary support sentences in the paragraph on Tutankhamen to see how the addition of secondary supports, drawn from our original list of supporting sentences, provides details that make the primary supports—and indirectly the controlling idea—more convincing. In the outline that follows, each primary support is reinforced by two secondary supports:

Topic Sentence: When the British archeologist Howard Carter excavated the tomb of the Pharoah Tutankhamen, he discovered an astonishing treasure of ancient Egyptian artwork.

    Primary Support 1: The antechamber of the tomb was filled with furniture, statues and carvings, and chests containing beautiful objects.

        Secondary Support 1a: In the center of the antechamber was a golden throne with arms in the form of winged serpents.

Secondary Support 1b: Near the throne were intricately carved alabaster vessels and life-size black statues, probably portraying Tutankhamen.

Primary Support 2: On the mummy was found a gold burial mask.

Secondary Support 2a: The dazzling mask was inlaid with semiprecious stones and glass paste.

Secondary Support 2b: The gold burial mask was a perfect likeness of Tut.

Primary Support 3: On the walls of the tomb were a number of magnificent murals, brightly painted in red, yellow, black, and white.

Secondary Support 3a: The wall paintings depicted events in the king's afterlife.

Secondary Support 3b: One wall showed the baboon spirits of the funerary realm through which the dead king would pass.

With your outline of primary and secondary supports complete, you are ready to write the paragraph, refining your preliminary sentences as necessary. Below is a possible final product:

When the British archeologist Howard Carter excavated the tomb of the Pharoah Tutankhamen, he discovered an astonishing treasure of ancient Egyptian artwork. The antechamber of the tomb was crowded with splendid pieces of ancient furniture, statues and carvings of untold worth, and chests containing beautiful objects. A golden throne with arms in the form of winged serpents stood in the center of the room. Near it were intricately carved alabaster vessels and life-size black varnished statues, probably portraying Tutankhamen. On the mummy was perhaps the tomb's most precious treasure: a gold burial mask. Inlaid with semiprecious stones and glass paste, the mask was dazzling to behold. It was a perfect likeness of Tutankhamen's face. On the walls of the tomb were a number of magnificent murals, brightly painted in red, yellow, black, and white. The wall paintings depicted various events in the king's afterlife. One particularly interesting painting showed the baboon spirits of the funerary realm through which the dead king would pass.

The secondary supports add to the effectiveness of the paragraph by providing specifics that reinforce the primary supports. For instance, the secondary supports following primary support 1 provide specific examples of the furniture and objects in the antechamber of Tutankhamen's tomb. Once the reader can visualize some of these objects in detail, he or she has enough information to accept the assertion that "the antechamber . . . was crowded with splendid pieces of ancient furniture, statues and carvings of untold worth, and chests containing beautiful objects." Likewise, primary supports 2 and 3 gain credence when the burial mask and the wall paintings are described in more detail in the secondary support sentences that follow them. Together the primary and secondary supports provide the reader with considerable evidence that the tomb of Tutankhamen did house "an astonishing treasure of ancient Egyptian artwork."

In a carefully planned paragraph, primary and secondary supports work in a unified manner to develop the paragraph's controlling idea convincingly. Secondary support sentences provide specifics that reinforce the primary supports, and strong primary supports, in turn, lead the reader to accept the validity of the paragraph's controlling idea. The finished paragraph is effective because all of its sentences are unified in their support of the paragraph's controlling idea.

A Word of Caution: Digressions at the Secondary-Support Level. Since secondary supports relate only indirectly to the controlling idea of a paragraph, most problems in unity occur on the level of secondary support. Here it is easy to lose sight of the controlling idea and introduce facts or ideas which do not add relevant support. For this reason, you should take special care not to get off the track when you are selecting secondary supports. Make sure that you select secondary supports that effectively reinforce your primary supports and that do not digress into related areas. Remember: *Primary supports reinforce the controlling idea directly; secondary supports reinforce the primary supports and, indirectly, the controlling idea.*

As the following paragraph illustrates, a single digression on the level of secondary support can cause the writer to wander far from the topic sentence and thus destroy the unity of a paragraph.

(1) Soap operas deal with true-to-life problems. (2) Frequently depicted on soap operas, criminal acts such as murder and rape are problems which we all fear and may face, directly or indirectly, at some time in our lives. (3) Hundreds of murders occur weekly in the United States. (4) Rape, too, is a frequent crime which police and citizens in every major city try to combat and prevent. (5) Soap operas also show characters suffering from serious diseases, such as cancer, heart attack, and stroke, which many people actually must face. (6) One out of every four Americans will eventually suffer from cancer. (7) Many forms of cancer are curable if discovered during their early stages. (8) Fortunately, medical science has devised several tests which are effective in diagnosing cancer at an early stage. (9) Unfortunately, however, most people don't take the time to receive these important tests when they should. (10) If you know people who have symptoms that may indicate cancer,

be sure that they receive the proper medical attention. (11) Otherwise they may suffer the unhappy fate of some of the characters on television soap operas.

Until sentence 7, this paragraph proceeds effectively. Sentence 2 is a primary support which reinforces the controlling idea that soap operas *deal with true-to-life problems.* Sentences 3 and 4 are secondary supports that provide specific evidence in support of sentence 2. Sentence 5 brings up the next primary support dealing with disease, and it, in turn, is reinforced by the secondary support in sentence 6.

When the writer reaches sentence 7, however, he goes off track. Instead of providing additional secondary support for sentence 5, he wanders off into a discussion of curable forms of cancer, tests to detect cancer, and the folly of people who don't take such tests when they should. By this point the writer has wandered far from his topic sentence. In fact, by the end of the paragraph, both writer and reader have almost completely lost sight of its controlling idea. Because he did not structure his paragraph carefully, the writer of this paragraph has allowed a single digression on the level of secondary support to lead him away from the controlling idea, undermining the unity of his work.

Much more effective is the following paragraph, which has the same topic sentence:

(1) Soap operas deal with true-to-life problems. (2) Frequently depicted on soap operas, criminal acts such as murder and rape are problems which we all fear and may face, directly or indirectly, at some time in our lives. (3) Hundreds of murders occur weekly in the United States. (4) Rape, too, is a frequent crime which police and citizens in every major city try to combat and prevent. (5) Soap operas also show characters suffering from serious diseases, such as cancer, heart attack, and stroke, which many people actually must face. (6) One out of every four Americans will eventually suffer from cancer. (7) An equal number of Americans experience heart attacks and strokes. (8) Divorce is another problem which soap operas frequently depict and which many people must deal with in the course of their lives. (9) Fifty percent of all marriages in America end in divorce. (10) Many people divorce more than once, and even those who don't get divorced may contemplate the possibility.

In this paragraph, the primary and secondary supports work together to explain and support the controlling idea. Sentences 2, 5, and 8 provide primary support for the controlling idea; the other sentences (including new sentences 7, 9, and 10) are secondary supports that effectively back up the primary supports and do not digress into related areas. The result is a unified paragraph which convincingly discusses what it set out to discuss.

So important are secondary supports to the overall unity of your paragraphs that even occasional digressions at the level of secondary support can seriously harm the unity of your writing, as in the following example:

> (1) Nashville, Tennessee, is the country-and-western-music capital of the world. (2) Most of the major country-and-western-music stars, including Minnie Pearl, Johnny Cash, and Tammy Wynette, own homes in Nashville. (3) Their homes, which have become symbols of Nashville's country-and-western heritage, are visited by thousands of admiring fans. (4) Many of these same fans also visit the home of Andrew Jackson, which is located just outside Nashville. (5) Several of Nashville's music halls boast festivals which attract country-and-western enthusiasts from around the world. (6) The internationally famous Opryland, U.S.A., set in a beautiful park, houses the Grand Ole Opry, where the stars of country-and-western music perform every Friday and Saturday night. (7) Other Nashville monuments include a restored colonial fort and a fine-arts museum. (8) Several small night spots on Nashville's famed Elliston Place offer less-established country-and-western artists the opportunity to gain public notice. (9) One of these, the Exit Inn, was recently popularized by Robert Altman in his film *Nashville,* an epic account of the country-and-western-music industry. (10) Some other famous films by Altman are *M*A*S*H, Buffalo Bill and the Indians,* and *The Wedding.*

This paragraph is carefully planned and structured at the primary-support level. The author has chosen three primary supports that back up the controlling idea that Nashville is *the country-and-western-music capital of the world:*

Primary Support 1: Most of the major country-and-western-music stars, including Minnie Pearl, Johnny Cash, and Tammy Wynette, own homes in Nashville.

Primary Support 2: Several of Nashville's music halls boast festivals which attract country-and-western enthusiasts from around the world.

Primary Support 3: Several small night spots on Nashville's famed Elliston Place offer less-established country-and-western artists the opportunity to gain public notice.

However, some of the secondary supports the writer has supplied are unrelated to the controlling idea and have little or nothing to do with the primary supports. The reader wonders, for example, what Andrew Jackson's home has to do with Nashville as the country-and-western-music capital of the world; or why the writer chose to mention that a visitor to Nashville can see a restored colonial fort and a fine-arts museum; or why the writer listed three films by Robert Altman which have nothing to do with Nashville or with country-and-western music. These digressions distract the reader and make the paragraph far less effective than it might have been had they been eliminated or replaced.

SUMMARY

1. Often primary supports, particularly those that provide support for unfamiliar or complex controlling ideas, require additional details or explanation to be convincing to the reader.

2. The sentences in a paragraph which reinforce a primary support by supplying additional details or explanation are called *secondary supports*. They constitute the third level of generality (see Chapter 1).

3. Unlike primary supports, secondary supports do not reinforce the controlling idea directly. Instead, they relate directly to a sentence of primary support. By adding information which helps make a primary support believable to the reader, they *indirectly* support the paragraph's controlling idea.

4. Since secondary supports relate only indirectly to the controlling idea of a paragraph, most problems in unity occur on the level of secondary support, where it is easy to lose sight of the controlling idea.

5. When you choose the secondary supports for your paragraph, be sure that they effectively reinforce your sentences of primary support. Do not use secondary supports that simply digress into related areas.

6. Even occasional digressions on the level of secondary support can seriously harm the effectiveness of your writing.

EXERCISES

I. For each of the following paragraphs, identify the topic and the controlling idea expressed in the topic sentence. Then decide whether the remaining sentences offer primary support or secondary support. If any sentence fails to support the controlling idea either directly as primary support or indirectly as secondary support, delete it.

    A. (1) Students who need part-time jobs should consider becoming a waiter or waitress. (2) The working hours in a restaurant are ideally suited to a student's schedule. (3) Most restaurants operate between the hours of 5:00 and 10:00 P.M., after students have finished their classes and have had time to do their assignments for the following day. (4) Students should always hand in their assignments on time, or they run the risk of lowering their grades. (5) Since restaurants don't expect their help to work more than two or three days a week, students who work as waiters or waitresses have more than enough free time to complete papers and projects on their days off. (6) The salary of a waiter or waitress is usually higher than what students can earn in other part-time jobs and is normally enough to pay for living expenses. (7) Expensive restaurants pay as much as $5.00 per hour to their waiters and waitresses, who also have the opportunity to earn as much as $75.00 per night in tips. (8) Even in small, inexpensive establishments, students who work as waiters or waitresses can usually earn $2.00 to $3.00 per hour plus tips—and no one can complain about that!

B. (1) London is a city of historical splendor. (2) Westminster Abbey, a Gothic structure built during the thirteenth century, is 531 feet long and almost 102 feet high. (3) Its architectural highlights include a splendid nave, special chapels, and a magnificent choir loft, all created by skilled artists and masons. (4) Many of Britain's most distinguished men, including Geoffrey Chaucer, Alfred Tennyson, Robert Browning, Isaac Newton, and Charles Darwin, are buried in Westminster Abbey. (5) Big Ben, a famous clock located on the tower of the Houses of Parliament, is a historic landmark in itself. (6) The ringing of its thirteen-and-one-half-ton bell, hung in 1858, has marked the passing of some of Britain's most historic hours. (7) Also in London is Buckingham Palace, which has been the royal family's home for over a hundred years. (8) Within the palace are a throne room where many historic events have taken place and an impressive staircase where visiting royalty have traditionally been received by the British monarch. (9) Queen Elizabeth is, of course, unlikely to talk with tourists, but it's worth a trip to Buckingham Palace anyway.

C. (1) If a wooden pool cue is to remain an accurate piece of equipment, it must be properly cared for. (2) The tip, or crown, of the cue should be kept rough and well chalked. (3) Keeping the tip of the cue in good condition helps prevent it from slipping when it strikes the ball. (4) The first eight inches of the cue's shaft should be rubbed with steel wool and kept covered with a layer of baby powder. (5) This procedure keeps oil and residue from collecting at the end of the stick and producing unnecessary friction. (6) Excess friction can severely impair the speed and accuracy of a pool shot. (7) In addition, the cue stick should be kept away from extreme heat and dampness. (8) Heat and moisture cause the stick to warp, making shooting a ball on center difficult. (9) For this reason, wooden pool cues should be kept in a case when not in use. (10) Cue cases reduce exposure to heat and moisture.

D. (1) There are three popular fallacies concerning Egyptian pyramids. (2) First, they were not built by slaves but by farmers. (3) During the spring, when the Nile overflowed its banks and flooded adjacent farms, farmers who could not till their fields were hired by the pharaoh to work on the construction of the pyramids. (4) These workers were paid in food and were free to quit whenever they wished. (5) Second, the pyramids weren't, as some people think, built by ancient astronauts as landmarks for flying saucers. (6) They were built as memorials to the pharaohs who were buried within them. (7) Third, pyramids were not built as sturdily as most people imagine. (8) The reason that they have survived for so long is the lack of humidity and rainfall in the Egyptian climate. (9) If the pyramids had been built in a climate like Michigan's, they would have been a heap of decayed and scattered stones by now.

E. (1) The Zugspitze Mountain in southern Germany is an ideal place to visit if one wishes to have a wondrous view of the Bavarian Alps and their neighboring scenery. (2) Standing on the peak of this mountain and facing east, one has a breathtaking view of the many snow-capped mountains that form the Bavarian Alps. (3) These mountains are covered with tall pines and thick firs which stand straight and stretch up to the sunny blue sky. (4) Turning to the north, one can look down upon the picturesque village of Garmisch. (5) Its many church steeples and quaint houses surrounded by high mountains give it a look of both beauty and tranquility. (6) During World War II, some important battles were fought near Garmisch. (7) Most people, however, have wisely put the war behind them and are more concerned with enjoying the present than with rehashing history. (8) Facing west and looking out into the distance, one can see the Neuschwanchstein Castle. (9) This giant castle, standing lonely in the mountains, has great walls and huge towers that give it a magical look all its own. (10) Turning southward, one can observe the beautiful Austrian Alps. (11) These mountains look as though they were sleeping giants covered with glistening blankets of powdered snow.

F. (1) Beyond a doubt, Muhammad Ali is "the greatest" heavyweight boxer ever to enter the ring. (2) No other boxer has successfully won and regained the heavyweight title three times. (3) Floyd Patterson won the title twice, but when he challenged "the champ" to a match, Patterson was knocked cold by Ali's powerful fists. (4) Furthermore, no other boxer has made a successful comeback after a two-year layoff. (5)

Jim Jeffers and Joe Louis tried but failed. (6) Finally, Ali has done more to popularize this sport than has any other heavyweight boxer, with the possible exception of Jack Dempsey. (7) His flamboyant personality and exuberant antics have captured the imagination of millions of Americans. (8) As a result, Ali's fights consistently break all records for the number of television viewers watching an individual sports event.

II. Supply two secondary supports for each of the following primary supports. Be certain that each secondary support reinforces its primary support and doesn't simply digress onto a related topic suggested by the primary support. Again, keep in mind that while secondary supports relate only indirectly to the controlling idea, their ultimate function is to add support to the controlling idea.

Model:

Topic Sentence: Different kinds of insurance offer different kinds of protection.

    Primary Support 1: Life insurance provides financial assistance to the family of the insured in the event of his or her death.

        Secondary Support 1a: The insured can provide for a sum to be paid to dependents in case of death.

        Secondary Support 1b: He or she can also plan to arrange an annuity for offspring.

    Primary Support 2: Health insurance is designed to pay medical bills if the insured becomes ill enough to require treatment.

        Secondary Support 2a: Standard medical insurance covers most of a family's hospital bills.

        Secondary Support 2b: Additional medical plans can provide further coverage.

    Primary Support 3: Disability insurance supplements or pays in full the salary of the insured if he or she becomes disabled or ill and cannot work.

        Secondary Support 3a: Disability insurance usually pays the worker injured on the job a percentage of his income.

        Secondary Support 3b: But there are types of disability that pay the injured his full income.

A. *Topic Sentence:* Job applicants should always look their best for an interview.

> *Primary Support 1:* Job candidates should wear clothes which are pleasant and tasteful. *Nice shirt, pants, t,*
>
> *Primary Support 2:* In addition, job candidates should make sure that they look clean and well groomed. *comb hair, washed*
>
> *Primary Support 3:* Above all, job candidates should appear cheerful, relaxed, and cooperative. *smile*

B. *Topic Sentence:* Americans are constantly being induced to spend their money.

> *Primary Support 1:* Billboards and magazine ads bombard us with slogans which promise happiness and fulfillment if we buy this or that product.
>
> *Primary Support 2:* Coupons and sales entice us to buy products and services which we often don't really need.
>
> *Primary Support 3:* Television commercials condition us to think that we can't live without the things they advertise.

C. *Topic Sentence:* People marry for a variety of reasons.

> *Primary Support 1:* Some people marry for companionship.
>
> *Primary Support 2:* Others marry because they want children.
>
> *Primary Support 3:* But the majority of people marry because they are in love.

D. *Topic Sentence:* Anyone who enters the field of politics must be prepared to face the scrutiny of the public.

> *Primary Support 1:* Because politicians are considered celebrities, the most trivial events in their personal lives attract public attention.
>
> *Primary Support 2:* Recently passed legislation requires candidates for public office to make their financial records public, and these records often become the subject of public controversy.
>
> *Primary Support 3:* Even the families of politicians must sacrifice their privacy when one of their members enters politics.

E. *Topic Sentence:* Television has something for everyone.

> *Primary Support 1:* Some programs are specially designed to provide entertainment and instruction for children of all ages.
>
> *Primary Support 2:* Lighthearted comedies and action-packed dramas cater to individuals who wish to escape from their everyday problems.

Primary Support 3: For the more discriminating viewer, television offers self-help programs, artistic productions, and carefully researched documentaries and specials.

How Much Support Is Enough?

A perplexing yet important problem you will encounter as you write is deciding how much supporting evidence to use in each paragraph. Once you have studied your list of potential supporting statements and focused on those which you may wish to use to develop and support your controlling idea, you face the problem of deciding how many primary supports are needed and, even more difficult, how many, if any, secondary supports should be included for each primary support.

There are no set rules to follow. As writer, you must decide for yourself how many primary and secondary supports are necessary to back up the controlling idea of your paragraph. With experience, you will learn that the number of primary and secondary supports needed varies from paragraph to paragraph. Various combinations of primary and secondary supports can produce an effective paragraph.

In deciding on the pattern of supporting statements to use in a paragraph, keep in mind that your goal in writing the paragraph is to convince the reader that your controlling idea is valid, as you contracted to do in the topic sentence. This means that you must use enough primary supports to develop your controlling idea fully and convincingly and enough secondary supports to guarantee that your reader will accept your primary supports.

But how much support is "enough"? Your first and most important task is to decide how many primary supports are needed to develop and support your controlling idea effectively. In some instances, the controlling idea itself may dictate the appropriate number. The following topic sentences are cases in point:

A career in psychiatry demands *patience, understanding,* and *skill.*

Four major factors contributed to the downfall of the Roman Empire.

Regular exercise *relieves tension, strengthens the muscles,* and *reduces the risk of heart disease.*

Benjamin Franklin will long be remembered for his achievements as *statesman, inventor, printer,* and *writer.*

Winning at pinball requires *strategy* and *precision.*

Having one's wisdom teeth removed can be a *frightening* and *painful* experience.

When potting chrysanthemums, one should follow *three basic steps.*

Loneliness and *fear* are *two major reasons* that the suicide rate among college students is high.

In each of these sentences, the italicized words suggest to the reader that a certain number of primary supports will follow, and it is the writer's responsibility to organize the paragraph along those lines.

Not every paragraph you write, however, will have a topic sentence that commits you to a definite number of primary supports; for those paragraphs that don't, you must decide for yourself how many are needed. In general, when you are in doubt about how many primary supports to include, you should use at least three. One point of primary support is usually inadequate reinforcement for the controlling idea unless the evidence it presents, when amplified through secondary supports, is overwhelmingly convincing. Two points of primary support are often enough to back up an idea—but if some of your readers don't accept one of your supports, the effectiveness of the paragraph will be weakened. Three points of primary support usually provide enough evidence to convince your readers that what you claim in your topic sentence is valid.

The following topic sentence and three primary supports illustrate this principle:

Topic Sentence: One should think twice before moving into a mobile home.

> *Primary Support 1:* Most mobile homes are too cramped to provide adequate living space.
>
> *Primary Support 2:* Furthermore, many mobile-home owners discover too late that trailers lack privacy.
>
> *Primary Support 3:* Finally, even well-constructed mobile homes aren't sturdy enough to support the activities of the average occupants.

If a paragraph with this topic sentence included only one or two of the primary supports above, many readers might remain unconvinced that "one should think twice before moving into a mobile home."

Keep in mind that using three primary supports is a useful guideline but not a hard-and-fast rule. As we have mentioned, in some cases it is adequate to use two primary supports (or even one) if each is sufficiently convincing and adequately backed up by secondary supports. In other cases, it may be appropriate to use more than three primary supports, either because you have additional points that you feel are too important to leave out or because you have little or no information to add at the level of secondary support. Be wary, however, of weighing your paragraph down with so much supporting evidence that your writing becomes dense and tedious to your reader.

For many students, knowing how many (if any) secondary supports to use is more difficult than deciding on the number of primary supports. Keep in mind this simple rule: Secondary supports are necessary to back up any primary supports that you feel your readers are unlikely to accept without additional explanation.

If your primary support is a straightforward and specific statement of fact, you probably don't need to develop it with secondary supports. The following paragraph on Daniel Boone, for example, consists only of a topic sentence and a series of primary supports of this type:

> (1) The Daniel Boone of history differs greatly from the Daniel Boone of legend. (2) The historical Daniel Boone never "kilt a b'ar" with his knife. (3) He didn't discover Kentucky, and he didn't write an autobiography. (4) Although people say that Daniel Boone was well over six feet tall, in reality he stood five feet five inches in his stocking feet. (5) The legendary Daniel Boone was motivated only by humanitarian concerns, but the real Daniel Boone was a land speculator whose get-rich-quick schemes nearly landed him in jail. (6) According to his own testimony, Boone killed only one Indian, not the hundreds legend says he did. (7) At the time of Boone's death, his neighbors did not associate the world-famous legends of his exploits with the old man of limited means and strength whom they knew, and he died lonely and neglected.

If, on the other hand, your primary support is assumption based on facts or ideas with which your readers might be unfamiliar, or if it is a statement of fact which requires additional information before it can be properly understood, then you should buttress it with the information your readers need to know in order to accept its validity.

The following paragraph outline, for example, illustrates the effective use of secondary support:

Topic Sentence: Rolling a cigarette is not as easy as cowboy stars make it seem.

> *Primary Support 1:* First, break up all lumps in the tobacco.
>
>> *Secondary Support:* Lumps can puncture the paper, with the result that smoke will not pass through the cigarette.
>>
>> *Secondary Support:* Lumps also burn at a different rate from properly packed tobacco.
>
> *Primary Support 2:* Next, obtain high quality papers recommended by a friend.
>
>> *Secondary Support:* Poor quality paper spoils the taste of the tobacco.
>>
>> *Secondary Support:* Many brand-name papers are of poor quality, and friends who have used different kinds of papers are the best source of information on which paper to purchase.

Primary Support 3: Next, form a pocket in the paper by creasing up approximately one quarter of the nongummed end.

Secondary Support: The pocket keeps the tobacco from spilling out of the wrapper.

Primary Support 4: Place the tobacco in the pocket, and spread it evenly across the length of the cigarette.

Secondary Support: If the tobacco is spread unevenly, the cigarette may not burn well.

Primary Support 5: Holding the filled paper with the thumb against the index and middle finger, roll the cigarette carefully.

Secondary Support: Using more than three fingers to roll the cigarette can produce a loosely rolled product, which is difficult to smoke.

The writer of this paragraph selected secondary supports thoughtfully, never allowing them to detract from the unity of the paragraph. The secondary supports reinforce and explain the primary supports, thereby making them more comprehensible.

Let's examine the structure of this paragraph more closely. The secondary supports which follow primary support 1 explain *why* lumps should be removed from any tobacco used in the making of cigarettes. Once the reader has read the secondary supports, the reasons for following the writer's instructions become clear. The secondary supports which follow primary support 2 explain why friends are the best source of information on the kind of cigarette paper to purchase and why the quality of the paper is important. Primary supports 3, 4, and 5, unlike 1 and 2, are each followed by only one secondary support. This is because one sentence was adequate to explain why the instructions in the primary support sentences should be followed.

If you are having trouble structuring the primary and secondary supports in your paragraphs and elect to follow a pattern of three primary supports for each topic sentence, you may find it helpful to use *two* sentences of secondary support to reinforce each primary support. In this way, you will be certain of having enough primary support for your controlling idea and enough secondary support to reinforce your primary supports. The basic structure for a paragraph of this sort is as follows:

SENTENCE 1:   *TOPIC SENTENCE*

SENTENCE 2:   PRIMARY SUPPORT 1

SENTENCE 3:   Secondary Support

SENTENCE 4:   Secondary Support

SENTENCE 5:   PRIMARY SUPPORT 2

SENTENCE 6:   Secondary Support

SENTENCE 7:   Secondary Support

SENTENCE 8:   PRIMARY SUPPORT 3

SENTENCE 9:   Secondary Support

SENTENCE 10:   Secondary Support

The paragraph on Tutankhamen's tomb (page 33) follows this pattern. So, too, does the following version of the paragraph on mobile homes (page 43), fully developed here by the use of secondary supports:

(1) One should think twice before moving into a mobile home. (2) Most mobile homes are too cramped to provide adequate living space. (3) Normal-size furniture barely fits into the narrow confines of the mobile home. (4) Shins and ankles are easily bruised on the protruding corners of end tables and other furnishings which crowd passageways. (5) Furthermore, many mobile-home owners discover too late that trailers lack privacy. (6) Footsteps echo loudly from one end of a trailer to the other, especially during the night, when normal sounds become amplified in the quiet. (7) Television, stereo music, and voices carry through the thinly paneled walls of the mobile home, sometimes into the home adjacent to it in the trailer park. (8) Finally, even well-constructed mobile homes aren't sturdy enough to support the activities of the average occupants. (9) Lacking a strong foundation, mobile homes gradually sink into the ground, causing doors to hang awry and furniture to shift. (10) Storms frequently ravage mobile homes, and even a washing machine on spin cycle can cause a mobile home to jump and wobble.

Without secondary supports, this paragraph would not be as convincing to the reader. The addition of secondary supports makes the primary supports more believable, thereby reinforcing the controlling idea.

As you become more confident in your writing, you may wish to experiment with different arrangements of primary and secondary supports. We by no means wish to discourage you from doing so now if you feel that you have enough understanding of paragraph unity and structure to know when and how primary and secondary supports should be used. As long as your paragraphs are unified and adequately developed, they can follow whatever arrangement of supporting statements you desire to use. The important thing is that you understand the nature and purpose of primary and secondary supports and that you realize the importance of developing your paragraphs according to a carefully planned system of support.

SUMMARY

1. As a writer, you must learn to decide how many primary and secondary supports are needed to reinforce the controlling idea of your paragraphs.
2. Every paragraph should contain enough primary supports to back up the controlling idea fully and convincingly, and it should have enough secondary supports to guarantee that the reader will accept its primary supports.
3. Sometimes the controlling idea of a paragraph will suggest or even dictate the number of primary supports which should be used in the paragraph.
4. When you are in doubt about how many primary and secondary supports to use in a paragraph, a good rule of thumb is to use three primary supports, and two secondary supports for each primary support.

EXERCISES

I. Write a paragraph using one of the following topic sentences. In your paragraph, use three primary supports and follow each primary support with two secondary supports. Make sure that each of your primary supports adds direct support to the paragraph's controlling idea and that your secondary supports back up the primary supports which they follow.

A. Preparing a Thanksgiving dinner involves more than just roasting a turkey.
B. Not all students want the same things from a college education.
C. Clothes often reflect the personalities of the people who wear them.
D. Deciding to have children requires serious thought.
E. Most commuters can benefit from joining a car pool.
F. History sometimes repeats itself.
G. Different kinds of cars suit the needs of different kinds of people.
H. Newspaper columnists should have the right to keep their sources secret.

II. Write paragraphs on two of the following topics. Use whatever arrangement of primary and secondary supports you feel most effectively supports your controlling idea. After you have written each paragraph, underline all sentences which function as primary supports. Make certain that each of your primary supports relates directly to the controlling idea of the paragraph and helps to support that idea effectively. Then make certain that your secondary supports back up the primary supports which they follow. Feel free to alter the topics in whatever manner you see fit. Instead of "disco dancing," for example, you may choose to write on waltzing or square dancing.

A. disco dancing   F. fast-food restaurants
B. *Star Wars* (the movie)   G. marijuana
C. grades   H. home gardening
D. pinball   I. slogans
E. pornography   J. sex symbols

III. Plan and write a unified paragraph on a topic of your own choosing. Use whatever arrangement of primary and secondary supports you feel best develops your controlling idea, and make certain that every sentence in the paragraph directly or indirectly supports the controlling idea.

Chapter 4

Methods of Development

In Chapter 3 you learned that all of the sentences in a paragraph must support, either directly or indirectly, the controlling idea expressed in your topic sentence. There are, however, a number of ways to develop support for your controlling idea so that your readers will be persuaded of its validity.

In this chapter, we are going to discuss six methods of developing an expository paragraph. You should become familiar with each so that you can organize and shape your supporting evidence in the way that is *most effective* for making the point that you wish to put across. The six methods are as follows:

1. Example
2. Definition
3. Comparison and contrast
4. Classification and division
5. Cause and effect
6. Process analysis

These six methods have been used by good writers for centuries. In fact, you will find that one or another of these methods has been used in practically all of the sample paragraphs included in this book and in many well-written paragraphs you will come across elsewhere in your reading.

The reason these methods of development have been so widely used is that they communicate ideas effectively. And they communicate effectively because they represent ways in which our minds naturally work when we wish to provide information and support our views. When we state that something is true, we are likely to give examples to support what we assert. Or we may define something to make it—or a statement about it—clear. Or we may compare or contrast two or more items to make their relative merits or characteristics clear. We often want to show why something came about or what its effects will be. And we often need to explain how something works. In other words, you would use these methods even if you didn't study them because they represent thought processes that come naturally to all of us. But study of the methods will show you how to use each effectively and how to select the one that will best serve you in getting a particular idea across convincingly.

Example

Example is probably the simplest method of development. In using it, the writer selects examples to support the controlling idea of the paragraph. In the following paragraph, the writer has supported a controlling idea—that "smoking *is hazardous to health*"—by giving examples of various types of health hazards that smoking may bring about:

> According to information collected by the American Cancer Society and other health-related organizations, smoking is hazardous to health. The rate of lung and throat cancer is far greater in cigarette smokers than in nonsmokers. Men who smoke pipes have a higher incidence of lip and mouth cancer than those who have never smoked a pipe. Moreover, smokers are more likely to experience heart attacks, ulcers, bronchitis, and emphysema than are nonsmokers. Recent research has uncovered the fact that women who smoke during pregnancy are more likely to have miscarriages than are women who don't smoke. Finally, babies born of smoking mothers are usually below average in weight.

The controlling idea of this paragraph, expressed in the first sentence, makes a statement evaluating a very popular habit. Thereafter, the writer gives explicit examples to support the assertion that smoking is hazardous to health:

1. The chance of having throat and lung cancer is greater for cigarette smokers.
2. The chance of having lip and mouth cancer is greater for pipe smokers.
3. The chance of having heart attacks, ulcers, bronchitis, or emphysema is greater for smokers.
4. The chance of having a miscarriage is greater for the smoking woman.

5. The weight of babies born of smoking mothers is usually lower than that of babies born of nonsmoking mothers.

Each of these examples effectively backs up the controlling idea of the paragraph.

When you develop a paragraph by giving examples, keep three important guidelines in mind:

1. *Be sure that your examples are appropriate.* The examples you use should clearly and directly support the controlling idea you state in your topic sentence.
2. *Be sure that your examples are specific.* Don't generalize. Don't be vague. Your examples should be concrete and clear.
3. *Use enough examples to convince the reader.* Usually three or more examples are needed. But, in the right situation, you may use one extended example which is developed in sufficient detail to provide adequate support.

Choosing Appropriate Examples

Be sure that every example you use illustrates your controlling idea directly and clearly. The following paragraph does not follow this advice to the fullest:

Violence in many forms exists in our society. Citizens are frequently robbed while walking on busy streets. They are robbed in their homes. Large companies that depend on computers are afraid that someone will push a few extra buttons on a computer and rob them of millions of dollars. Storeowners must maintain a constant vigil for shoplifters who remove food and other articles from their stores. Schools are often the target of vandals bent on destroying property. Schools also have to watch out for students who cheat on homework and exams.

The first two examples—of citizens being robbed on the streets or in their homes—are appropriate because violence frequently accompanies robberies. The example of vandalism in schools is also appropriate, for such vandalism is usually violent. The other examples, though, are of acts that may be criminal but are not necessarily violent. Robbery through manipulation of a computer does not involve violence, nor does shoplifting or cheating on homework and exams. The paragraph needs to be rewritten so that *all* of the examples point to the existence of violence in our society.

Here is the paragraph as the student revised it:

Violence in many forms exists in our society. First of all, citizens are frequently assaulted and robbed on busy streets. In addition, they are sometimes threatened or injured in their homes by robbers looking for money or valuables. What is more, criminals intent on making a getaway may shoot the driver of a car and steal the car. A woman passenger in the car may be raped. Furthermore, schools are often the target of vandals bent on destroying property. And fires set in public buildings or residences sometimes result in injuries or deaths.

In this paragraph every example helps to support the controlling idea that *violence in many forms exists in our society.* The addition of the words "assaulted," "threatened," and "injured" helps to relate the statements about robberies *directly* to violence. Three new examples—a shooting during a car theft, the rape of a passenger, and injury or death resulting from arson—give further support to the controlling idea.

Including Specifics

All of your examples should be made concrete and clear by the use of specifics. Not only is the following student paragraph too brief to be convincing, but the examples it contains are much too vague:

> The Bible presents a great variety of literary genres. It includes books that deal with history. It offers dramas as interesting as many dramas today. In the Bible, one can read numerous biographies. The Bible also offers poetry in many of its books.

The writer does offer some appropriate examples: she lists as literary genres what she calls "history," "drama," "biography," and "poetry." But the examples are not specific enough. The average reader may not be aware that the Bible does in fact contain many kinds of literature. Therefore, in order to provide adequate support for the view expressed in the topic sentence, the writer should name specific books of the Bible that contain the literary genres she has listed and supply other supporting details.

Following is an improved version of the same paragraph:

> The Bible contains a great variety of literary genres that provide us with some very interesting reading. It gives us history in Kings and in other books. It gives us drama in the Book of Job. In fact, the Book of Job has been turned into a well-known modern play, and Job has become one of the best-known characters in all literature. The Bible also contains several biographies. The best known is, of course, that of Jesus. In the first four books of the New Testament, there are four versions of the life of Jesus, recounting the events of his life from his birth and childhood to his crucifixion. The Bible also offers poetry in many of its books, but the psalms are the most famous of its poems. They have been chanted in monasteries and churches and learned by heart by men and women through the ages.

Providing Enough Examples

Using Three or More Examples. In developing a paragraph by the use of examples, the writer does not have to use every appropriate example he or she can think of. But the writer should use enough examples to be convincing. A good rule of thumb is to use three or more examples, each of which constitutes a primary support. As can be seen in the following paragraph, written by a student, two examples are usually not enough:

> There are many educational television programs for children that involve no violence at all. Many constructive programs, such as "Grammar Rock" and "Multiplication Rock," are presented on the networks at a time when children can watch them. "Grammar Rock" teaches children about nouns, pronouns, adverbs, and adjectives. Thus, it helps a child to understand language. "Multiplication Rock" teaches children how to multiply and divide. Thus, it reinforces what a child studies in arithmetic.

The two examples given of educational programs for children are not enough to rid many people of the idea that most children's television programs tend to be violent. The writer must present more examples to validate the controlling idea.

The following paragraph is more convincing because it includes more examples:

> There are many educational television programs for children that involve no violence at all. "Grammar Rock" teaches children about nouns, verbs, adjectives, and adverbs. "Multiplication Rock" teaches them how to multiply and divide. "Sesame Street" teaches children many basic skills, such as counting and spelling. Other programs, like "Captain Kangaroo" and "Mister Rogers' Neighborhood," give children information about the world around them and also teach them how to be unselfish and how to get along with others.

Although the writer of this paragraph could have used more examples, he uses enough to make his point convincing. We are given five examples of nonviolent children's programs and are told a number of ways in which the programs are educational.

It should also be noted that while the examples in this particular paragraph are all appropriate and specific, none is discussed in much detail. A practical guideline is that the less you develop each example, the more examples you will need to back up your controlling idea. Two or three examples must be supported by detailed secondary supports to be as convincing as five examples discussed only briefly.

Using One Extended Example. There are occasions when one example very fully developed may carry the weight of many that are more briefly stated. A good illustration of the use of one extended example is the paragraph which follows:

> Although they may appear friendly, the bears in Yellowstone National Park can be extremely dangerous and destructive. I learned this lesson on a camping trip last summer. A friend of mine and I were setting up camp close to a dry river bed in a forlorn canyon when our attention was directed toward two large bears that were peacefully walking down a narrow path. Suddenly the huge animals stopped, gave us a curious look, and then turned slowly and disappeared into the forest. Unafraid, we continued our work. Afterward, we built a fire and cooked meat and eggs for supper. Being inexperienced campers, we left food scraps—an obvious attraction for wild animals—around the campsite when we retired for the night. Thirty minutes later we awoke to the sound of growls and crunches. Two bears were eating the abandoned scraps of food and tearing at our partially filled knapsacks. Seeking safety, we climbed a nearby pine tree and watched helplessly as the bears completely demolished our camp in an apparent search for more food. After this destructive action, the bears, to our surprise, walked into the forest, completely ignoring us. Had we antagonized them, though, they might very well have attacked us.

The controlling idea of this paragraph, communicated in the topic sentence, is that "the bears in Yellowstone National Park *can be extremely dangerous and destructive.*" "I learned this lesson on a camping trip last summer" serves as primary support for the opening statement. The extended example or narrative that follows is actually a secondary support, although it contains a series of events. This variation on the g–s paragraph can be very effective—especially if you draw on personal experience.

SUMMARY

1. In a paragraph developed by the use of examples, all the examples should be appropriate—that is, they should support the controlling idea of the paragraph.
2. All examples should be specific.
3. The writer should use enough examples to make the paragraph convincing. Three or more examples are usually needed, but one extended example may sometimes be effective.

EXERCISES

I. Read the following topic sentences; then think of a number of examples (preferably more than three) which you can use to support each one. Be sure that your examples are appropriate and specific. If any of the topics lends itself to development by the use of one extended example, explain how you would develop this example.

   A. Television commercials are just as much a part of our lives as Mom's apple pie.

   B. Most television commercials are an insult to human intelligence.

   C. Space exploration has given us many small miracles.

   D. Citizens who report sighting an unidentified flying object risk bringing ridicule upon themselves.

   E. Prejudice comes in many forms.

   F. Humans have always wanted to fly.

   G. Some people are their own worst enemies.

   H. Americans have many patriotic songs.

II. Read each of the following paragraphs carefully. Write down each sentence that begins a new example; then list the number of examples contained in each paragraph. State whether or not each example is *appropriate* and *specific*.

   A. There are many ways to cut the costs of rising grocery bills. Purchasing store brands instead of the popular brands advertised on television and in magazines saves money, since the cost of advertising does not have to be included in the cost of store-brand items. Peanut butter and canned vegetables with store-brand labels usually are of the same quality as widely advertised national brands. Another way to make pennies count is to clip money-saving coupons from newspapers and to watch for weekly specials. Buying in quantity can also cut per-item expenses. And shopping for fresh fruits and vegetables when they are in season can result in considerable savings for the shopper. Finally, shoppers who bring marketing lists and stick to them avoid the temptation of buying on impulse and thus avoid spending money that they otherwise would not spend.

   B. Watching different students handle the same type of pressure—the pressure of taking a final exam in English composition—provides a fascinating study of human behavior. One student stares vacantly at the blackboard, hoping and praying that an idea will suddenly pop into his mind. After a short while, an idea does form; the student jots down the idea, and after a couple of minor revisions he finishes the paper. Another student gets to work on her paper, writes half a page, then decides to change the subject. She starts all over again. Perhaps the pressure of taking an exam so unnerves her that she is unable to stay on one subject and finish the paper. Still another student, whose former school experience has not included theme writing, looks desperately around the room and, upon seeing everyone else concentrating, tries to concentrate himself. But he begins to sweat and is immobilized for a minute or so. Finally, he realizes that he has only ten minutes left in which to perform, and in desperation he begins to write down a few disconnected sentences. Still another student, one in the front of the room, writes feverishly, reads the result nervously, then crushes the paper into a ball and starts all over. One particularly sly student, though, decides that the best way to write the paper is to rattle on about some trivial subject and pretend that he is turning out a good paper. He finds that reporting on the effects of pressure on his fellow students reduces tension and keeps him from becoming a victim of that pressure himself.

C. Would you believe that something as small as the peanut could have hundreds of uses? Every year millions of peanuts are turned into peanut butter, one of America's favorite foods. Roasted peanuts are salted and eaten as snacks or used in candies and bakery products. Salad oils and margarines are made from peanuts. Farmers use peanut vines, hulls, and skins as feed for their animals. Other products made from the peanut are cosmetics, soap, packing oil, medicines, and even explosives. In fact, there are more than three hundred uses for the peanut plant and its fruit.

D. According to ancient superstitions, moles on the body reveal a person's character and foretell the future. Some moles reveal strengths and weaknesses of character. A mole on the back of the neck indicates that the bearer is a spendthrift. Moles on both sides of the neck reveal extreme stubbornness. A mole on the left knee is a sure indication that the bearer is unwise in business matters. In fact, a mole on any part of the leg indicates that one is both indolent and wasteful. A mole over the left eyebrow hints of laziness as well as selfishness. If one meets someone with a mole on any finger, he should hold on to his wallet: according to superstition, the person is sure to be a crook. But a friend with a mole on his nose is strong of character and will always remain a true friend. In addition to revealing character, moles are said to foretell the future. There is an old saying, "A mole on the neck, money by the peck." If the mole is on the front of the neck, good luck may come from any source. A mole on the ear also brings good luck in the form of money. A mole over the right eyebrow means success in love, money, and career. A mole on the hand, however, is the most to be desired: it forecasts the good news that one will be talented, healthy, rich, and happy.

E. Representatives in Congress really enjoy the "gravy" provided by the American tax dollar. To start with, the salary itself is not bad. This January, our newly elected representative will go to Congress. His annual salary will be $57,500. In addition to his salary, he will receive fringe benefits galore. Available to him will be a $7,000 personal expense allowance and a $6,500 stationery allowance, together with an additional $5,000 postage allowance for mailing letters written on this free paper. Further advantages include thirty-three free round trips per year between his home and Washington, a free furnished office in Washington, and more than $250,000 for personal staffing and related expenses. In addition, the Congressman-elect will receive free plants and flowers from the botanical gardens and free medical care and drugs. He will also have access to a professionally staffed radio and television studio. Finally, he will be able to retire on a neat $35,000 per year pension.

F. In many ways the staff at this university has given me a hard time with my education. When I first arrived here three years ago from my native China, Mr. "N," in the Office for Foreign Students, lost my visa. Since then the staff and computers have given me innumerable occasions for worry and frustration. For three years in a row, the people in the registrar's office have sent me notices saying that I was not carrying a full-time load when, in fact, I was carrying a fourteen-hour load, two more hours than is required of full-time students. The office lists my birth date as August 1, 1954, but they insist that I am forty-eight years old. They say that I am a freshman, but I am really a junior. There are many other mistakes that they have made, but the one that takes the cake is their informing me, just last week, that I am an American Eskimo from Tunisia.

III. Write a paragraph on one of the following topics. Develop your topic sentence through the use of examples.

   A. body language
   B. celebrities
   C. shoes
   D. habits
   E. bottles
   F. bores
   G. villains
   H. faces

IV. Using example as your method of development, write a paragraph on a topic of your choosing. Be certain that your example or examples are appropriate and specific. And be certain that you use enough examples, or develop one example fully enough, to support your controlling idea adquately.

Definition

The second method of development is *definition.* A writer employs this method of development when he wants to thoroughly explain the meaning of a word, phrase, term, or concept for the reader. Definitions may be either *formal* or *informal.* We'll consider each of these.

Formal Definition

Formal definitions are the kind found in dictionaries. There are two parts to a formal definition. In the first part, the word being defined is assigned to a *class,* or larger category of related concepts. For example, the formal definition of the term *traffic light* would assign it to the class "electronically operated visual signal." The second part of the definition lists the characteristics that differentiate the item from other items in the same class, such as—in this case—a railroad semaphore. What sets a traffic light apart from other "electronically operated visual signals" is that it "controls the flow of road vehicle and pedestrian traffic." A complete formal definition of a traffic light, then, is "an electronically operated visual signal that controls the flow of road vehicle and pedestrian traffic."

The table that follows contains five terms that have been broken down into the two elements of formal definition: *class* and *differentiating characteristic(s).*

Term	Class	Differentiating Characteristics
chameleon	lizard	having the ability to change the color of its skin
minaret	slender tower	connected to a mosque, and the place from which a crier calls Moslems to prayer
graffiti	writing	on walls or public places
UFO	flying object	with unknown origin and identity
clone	offspring	reproduced from a cell of a single animal or plant

Any term that is placed in a class and then distinguished from other items in its class in terms of specific differences is defined by means of formal definition. In differentiating a term, you must be careful to make your definition narrow enough to ensure that it cannot cover any other terms from the same class.

In a paragraph, a formal definition may be used in one of two ways:

1. A formal definition may itself form the basis of the paragraph.
2. A formal definition may be used to clarify the controlling idea of a paragraph. In this method of paragraph development, the rest of the paragraph supports the controlling idea by showing that the definition fits the topic under discussion.

We'll look at each of these uses more closely.

Using a Formal Definition as the Basis of a Paragraph. A valid formal definition of the term *university* might be the following:

> A *university* is an institution of higher learning which includes one or more undergraduate schools or colleges, graduate programs leading to advanced degrees, and one or more professional schools.

The following paragraph is devoted to an expanded version of this formal definition:

> A *university* is an institution of higher learning that has three components. First, a university includes one or more undergraduate schools or colleges, such as a school of education and a college of arts and science. Second, a university offers graduate programs leading to advanced degrees. The graduate school of arts and science, in particular, grants M.A. and Ph.D. degrees. Finally, a university has one or more

professional schools under its jurisdiction. It may have, for example, a school of law or a school of medicine or—as is frequently the case—both. The law school grants J.D. or LL.B. degrees; the medical school grants M.D. degrees. Some universities, moreover, have schools of dentistry, veterinary medicine, architecture, and other professional areas.

This entire paragraph is a formal definition. The topic is the term *university,* and the controlling idea indicates that the term *university* belongs in the class "institutions of higher learning" and "has three components," which are its distinguishing characteristics. The remainder of the paragraph describes these components.

Sometimes in a paragraph using definition you may find it necessary to define more than one term. In defining one term, for instance, you may have to use another term which must be explained as well. It's best to define the second term as quickly and efficiently as possible, for it is not central to your plan. Thus, in a paragraph that includes a definition of a *motocross* as a "race against time by one motorcycle and driver through a course containing a number of hazards such as rough patches of ground and pylons," the writer must pause long enough to define *pylons* as "slender structures which mark the race course at various points, narrowing it and thus providing a challenge to the driver's skill." Having made it clear that pylons are obstacles between which a driver must steer, the writer can proceed with his work of defining *motocross.*

Using a Formal Definition to Clarify the Controlling Idea. A formal definition may also be used to clarify or explain a term that is vital to understanding a controlling idea. With this method, the topic sentence is followed by a definition, and the topic sentence and the defining sentence together function as a control for the paragraph. Support actually begins with the third sentence, and the rest of the paragraph aims to show that the topic under discussion fits the definition. For example, in a discussion of the suitability of calling an educational institution a *university* rather than a *college,* one might find the following paragraph:

> Pinkerton College deserves its new name of Pinkerton University. A *university* is an institution of higher learning that includes colleges, graduate programs leading to advanced degrees, and one or more professional schools. For the last twenty-five years, Pinkerton has had a college of liberal arts, a college of fine arts, a college of physical sciences and mathematics, and a college of education. Pinkerton offers graduate programs leading to the M.A. and M.S. degrees in the various colleges. Pinkerton has also had a distinguished medical school. And for the past twelve years it has had a school of law that is gaining a solid reputation in this part of the country. Thus, Pinkerton College has actually been a university for quite a long time—all it lacked was the name.

The idea the writer hopes to convey is that Pinkerton was already a university before it was officially called one. The best way to do this is to tell what a university is—that is, to define *university*—and then to present facts showing that the school in question conforms to the definition. By this method, the writer establishes the idea expressed in the topic sentence.

Informal Definition

A formal definition places the term being defined into a class, or category, and then lists the traits that distinguish that item from other items in the same class. An informal definition, on the other hand, gives the meaning of the term in a less structured manner. In informal definition, the rules used in formal definition may be relaxed. One may assign a term to a class, but the class does not have to be strictly precise. If, for example, one were to call a *dog* "man's best friend," one would be putting the term *dog* into the loose class "friend"—which would have no meaning in a zoological, formal definition of *dog*.

Many terms do not lend themselves to formal definition. Because everyday terms, such as *dog*, are so well known, informal definition of such terms is frequently more appropriate and meaningful than formal definition. Abstract terms, also, are often defined informally. Formal definitions of terms such as *patriotism, love,* or *hate* are infrequently called for and hard to make meaningful. One may define *patriotism* formally by calling it "loyalty" (class) "to one's native land" (differentiating characteristic), but this formal definition does not convey the spirit of patriotism, which is also important to an understanding of the term.

Although some terms require definition by the formal rather than the informal method (for example, *calorie* or *ion*), most terms may be defined by either method. In setting out to define a term, a writer must choose between these two types of definition. Making this choice involves two basic considerations: context and tone.

Context. If a paragraph using definition is to appear in a formal context, formal definition will most likely be called for. For example, in a textbook intended for use by a university class in architecture, the term *kitchen* would probably be placed in the class "room" and then be described according to architectural characteristics that distinguish it from other rooms in a house. Specific distinguishing characteristics would include the details that a student must consider in designing the kitchen of a house.

In a less formal context, the writer would find it more natural to use informal definition. In a general essay on the house one would not have to define *kitchen* formally because the term is well known to everyone. Instead, the writer would take an informal approach, bringing out some of the many connotations of the term *kitchen*. For instance, it might be defined in terms of the importance of this room to the American family: readers who are familiar with the formal meaning of the word would be made aware of other aspects of its significance.

Tone. The tone of any piece of writing conveys the author's attitude toward his material. If his attitude is impersonal and precise, he is likely to use formal definition when developing a paragraph by means of definition. If, on the other hand, the writer's attitude is personal, or if his intention is evaluative—that is, if he wishes to bring out the value or significance of the item under discussion—he will probably make use of informal definition.

In the following paragraph, for example, the writer conveys a personal attitude in an informal definition of the term *dog:*

> A dog is man's best friend. He is always there when you need a friend. He keeps you company when you are alone. I would have spent many difficult nights alone if it had not been for my dog. My dog forgives and forgets when I am moody and take my feelings out on him. He never holds a grudge against me. He just seems to understand. He is there to listen to my gripes when no one else has the time. A dog gives love and demands little in return.

While not all dogs and dog owners have this kind of relationship, most dog owners would agree that this informal definition reveals an important aspect of the meaning of the term *dog*.

There are no hard-and-fast rules for developing a paragraph by informal definition; the writer enjoys a great deal of freedom. The writer of the paragraph above simply made a series of statements showing the ways in which her dog was her "best friend." The point for you to keep in mind is that in any paragraph developed by informal definition, the topic sentence should state the special significance of the term to be discussed, and the rest of the paragraph should support the topic sentence.

SUMMARY

1. A formal definition of a term identifies the class to which the term belongs and the specific characteristics that differentiate it from other members of the class.
2. A formal definition may form the basis of a paragraph.
3. A formal definition may also be used to clarify the controlling idea

of a paragraph that is not primarily concerned with the definition itself. When used in this way, the definition of an important term in the topic sentence is interposed between the topic sentence and the rest of the paragraph.

4. Informal definition is less structured and precise than formal definition. It aims to bring out the special connotations of the term being defined.
5. Informal definition is often used to define abstract terms which do not lend themselves to satisfactory definition through formal definition, or to define everyday terms which are already well known.
6. The choice of formal or informal definition is determined by context and by the attitude of the writer toward his subject.

EXERCISES

I. Following are seven topic sentences that lend themselves to development by means of definition. Consider them carefully, and for each sentence write out the answers to questions A, B, C, and D.

    A. Should the paragraph be developed by formal or informal definition?

    B. If by formal definition, what term should be defined? Should the formal definition itself form the basis of the paragraph, or should the definition provide clarification of the controlling idea?

    C. If informal definition seems appropriate, what term should you define? What are the qualities you should bring out in order to give a clear impression of the object or idea being defined?

    D. Could the topic sentence be developed by both formal and informal definition?

Topic Sentences:

    (1) Weeds are worthless plants.
    (2) Microwave ovens provide the most efficient way to cook.
    (3) The pinball machine called "8-Ball" is a rip-off.
    (4) "Homemade" food is not always made entirely at home.
    (5) Fast-food restaurants are an essential part of modern living.
    (6) The gifted child is easy to identify if one knows what signs to look for.
    (7) We should all give the hamburger a round of applause.

II. In each of the following paragraphs, a student has attempted to develop a paragraph by means of definition. Read each paragraph carefully and answer the following questions:

A. Does the writer attempt to use formal or informal definition?

B. Is the attempt successful or not? Consider the following questions in your answer:

1. What term is being defined?

2. If the definition is formal, into what class does the author place the term? What are the distinguishing characteristics that set the item apart from other members of the class? Does the paragraph itself constitute a definition, or is the definition a clarification of the controlling idea followed by sentences that support the controlling idea?

3. If development is by informal definition, how does the writer go about making the reader grasp the special significance of the object or concept being defined?

Paragraphs:

A. *Sickle-cell anemia* is a disease in which red blood cells become sickle-shaped because of the malformation of the large oxygen-carrying molecule, hemoglobin. Although the malformation involves only a tiny part of the molecule, it causes a great reduction in the ability of the entire cell to carry oxygen. In addition, the distorted cells cannot pass through the capillaries. Instead, the sickle cells form clumps which can grow and collect, sometimes blocking important larger vessels and preventing whole sections of tissue from getting necessary oxygen. This causes cell death and can be excruciatingly painful for the victim. Another problem is the fact that the blocked vessels do not allow free passage of antibodies and other substances necessary for protection from diseases and repair of damaged tissue. Perhaps the greatest problem, though, concerns treatment: there is neither a cure nor a preventive for sickle-cell anemia. The disease is inherited, occurring most often in blacks, although members of other racial and ethnic groups may suffer from it. Because it is possible to carry the trait for the disease without being harmed by it, it is wise for all couples who are considering having children to be tested for the trait. Those people who do carry the gene for sickle-cell anemia should think carefully about the chances their children might have for a healthy life.

B. A *black hole* is not a hole at all. Rather, it is the remains of a star that in dying collapses on itself. As this happens, the star becomes dense enough to develop a very strong gravitational field, pulling in all matter surrounding it, including its former planets. As time goes on, the black hole becomes increasingly strong and dense as it "eats" more and more galactic matter. Eventually, it begins to migrate from one galaxy to another, its own gravity pulling it toward other bodies. When scientists first noticed these wandering phenomena, the black holes seemed to them to be areas containing a strong force but no matter—mysterious moving vacuums. Later, however, astronomers discovered that there was indeed a tremendous amount of matter in a black hole's center, which in volume might be no larger than the head of a pin.

C. Music can influence and express thoughts, feelings, and emotions. Have you ever been in a bad mood or feeling rather sad when a song suddenly came over the radio which made you feel even worse? Have you ever been in a good mood and feeling rather happy, when a song came over the radio which made you feel better? Many songs contain a mysterious force that releases listeners from reality and awakens the inner spheres of their emotions. So powerful is this force that people have always used music to convey their emotions to others, knowing that if, even for just an instant, the listener feels the flow of emotion from a memory or dream, the music maker has communicated with the listener on a profound level.

D. According to *Webster's, soul* is "a strong positive feeling (as of intense sensitivity and emotional fervor) conveyed esp. by American Negro performers," but this definition doesn't adequately explore the full meaning of soul. Soul is the manner of movement and motion that American blacks have inherited from their African ancestors. Soul is a unique style of body language that belongs to the black race alone. Soul encompasses repressed aspirations and suppressed potentials, exuberant emotions and heart-rending sadness, and all the idiosyncrasies peculiar to the black people. Soul is a birthright. It can't be imitated or acquired; only blacks possess it. To have it, one must be of African descent. Soul is the elusive, intangible inheritance of black Americans whose cultural identity is present in the very marrow of their bones.

E. Snow is a beautiful nuisance. Snowflakes fall from the sky with silent grace, and on the ground they can form a blanket that covers the earth's imperfections, but they can also cause trouble. A single, lovely, little, white, feather-light flake of snow cannot do much damage, but several million can combine to knock down power lines, bury cars, and cave in roofs. Snow also produces dangerous driving conditions, and it can leave cities and towns isolated and immobilized for weeks. Snow is a wolf in sheep's clothing.

F. A paragraph is a group of sentences organized to express a definite idea in a unified and orderly way. With some exceptions, a paragraph has three or more sentences—usually more. The first of these sentences introduces a topic and a controlling idea that requires explanation or support. The other sentences in a paragraph support the first sentence. They work together to support the paragraph's controlling idea, and they are arranged in the way that best achieves this end. The sentences in a paragraph fit together, like pieces of a puzzle, and the whole says something that its individual parts, taken separately, could never say.

III. Using either formal or informal definition, develop a paragraph on one of the following topics. Decide whether the paragraph can be developed better by formal or by informal definition. If you choose formal definition, first jot down the class to which the term belongs and the characteristics that make the item different from other members of the class. If you use informal definition, jot down the special qualities you wish to bring out. Then proceed.

    A. anger

    B. history

    C. brunch

    D. comic books

    E. sororities (or fraternities)

    F. mascots

    G. patriotism

    H. grass

    I. TSS (toxic shock syndrome)

IV. Write two paragraphs on a topic or topics of your own choice. Develop one by formal definition and the other by informal definition. You can use one topic for both paragraphs or two different topics. Be sure that the terms which you define lend themselves to the method of definition you have chosen.

Comparison and Contrast

A third method of paragraph development is comparison and contrast. Although the term *comparison* is often loosely used to refer to an evaluation of both likenesses and differences in two or more items, we will reserve it to refer to a consideration of likenesses only. When one considers likenesses between two or more items, one is *comparing* them; when one concentrates on differences, one is *contrasting* them. Understood in this sense, the two methods are, so to speak, two sides of the same coin. The techniques writers use in the two approaches are the same, and it is those techniques we will take a look at in this section.

Although in your reading you may find both comparison and contrast in the same paragraph, in a fairly short essay and in most single paragraphs, it is best to concentrate on either comparison or contrast and not attempt to cover both. Whether you compare or contrast will depend on whether the items being considered are substantially alike or unlike. It will also depend on your intention—that is, on whether you want to show similarities or differences. In some cases your instructor may specify whether to use comparison or contrast in a paragraph assignment. Most often, however, your task will be to consider two people, objects, or ideas carefully and to relate them in a paragraph. It will be up to you to examine their likenesses and differences and to decide which are important and more useful to discuss. You will then express your decision in a topic sentence which focuses the paragraph on either comparison or contrast.

We have seen that definition can be either formal or informal. When comparison or contrast is used to support and develop a paragraph's controlling idea, it, too, can be either formal or informal. Formal comparison and contrast are guided by specific rules that must be strictly adhered to. In informal comparison and contrast, those rules can be relaxed.

Formal Comparison and Contrast

Compare or Contrast Items in the Same Class. In formal comparison and contrast, the items you consider must be in the same *class*—that is, in the same related group or category. It makes no sense, for example, to compare an alligator and a banana, or, for that matter, to contrast them. It would be hard indeed to put these two items in the same class. On the other hand, it would make a great deal of sense to compare (or contrast) an alligator and a crocodile. These reptiles are related—and in fact many people confuse the two animals. A workable paragraph of comparison, then, might explain their similarities in some detail. If, on the other hand, you felt that readers would benefit more from a discussion of the differences between the two animals, contrast would be the appropriate method of development.

You might, too, profitably compare bus travel and air travel; both belong to the class "modes of travel." They may be compared and found to be alike in a number of ways. But since each has its own advantages, they can also be usefully contrasted. In a paragraph of formal comparison, you would focus on the similarities; in a paragraph of formal contrast, you would focus on the differences.

Identify a Class Sufficiently Narrow for Comparison or Contrast to be Meaningful. If the items being considered are not in a sufficiently narrow class, comparison or contrast becomes pointless. The two items discussed in the following paragraph, a Toyota Corolla and a Cadillac Eldorado, are both in the broad class "automobiles." Therefore, the student who wrote the paragraph felt that the contrast would be appropriate:

> There are many differences between a Toyota Corolla and a Cadillac Eldorado. The Toyota Corolla is an economy car. It averages thirty-five miles to a gallon of gas. The Cadillac Eldorado is a luxury car. It averages fifteen miles to a gallon. The Corolla has less leg room and is not as comfortable as the more spacious Eldorado. The list price of a new Corolla is approximately $5,000, while the list price of a new Eldorado is more than $15,000. Thus the differences between the two cars are decisive.

In this paragraph, developed through formal contrast, the topic sentence points to differences between the two cars. However, while the paragraph is technically a proper contrast between items in the same class (automobiles), the point made in the topic sentence and in the paragraph itself is not very significant because the cars are so far apart in price that few people would ever seriously consider the two together. A prospective buyer of a Toyota Corolla might more profitably compare or contrast this car with other cars in the moderate-price range.

Make the Basis or Bases* of Your Comparison or Contrast Clear. When you compare or contrast two items, you must have a good basis—or, what is often even better, several bases—on which to judge the items. In the paragraph contrasting the Toyota Corolla and the Cadillac Eldorado, the writer considered the cars on three bases: mileage per gallon of gas, comfort, and list price. If, instead of select-

---

*The word *bases,* pronounced "bayseez," is the plural form of the word *basis.*

ing a basis (or bases) for direct comparison or contrast, you randomly give facts first about one of the items and then about the other, the result will very likely be haphazard, as in the following paragraph:

> Many people travel by plane, many others by bus, but there are several differences between these two ways of traveling. Flying is easy on the traveler. You can fly across the United States in a few short hours. There are flight attendants to tend to your every need. You can have your meals served on the plane at no extra cost. Travel by bus is very common in the United States also. The new buses are much more comfortable than those which were used a few years ago. If you travel by bus, you really get to see the countryside. Also most buses are air-conditioned today.

The writer of this paragraph brings up several important factors in travel—comfort, speed, and sightseeing possibilities—but nowhere in the paragraph does he use any of these aspects as a basis for comparing or contrasting air and bus travel *directly*. For instance, we are given three reasons why flying is "easy" on the traveler—speed, attentive service, and no-extra-cost meals. We are not told anything, though, about service or meals on a bus or about relative traveling times. Moreover, the writer contrasts the comfort of bus travel today with that of a few years ago but does not say how the increased comfort on buses compares with the ease of flying. After reading this paragraph, one finds it difficult to come to any conclusion as to whether it is better to travel by bus or by plane.

Actually, most travelers would probably agree that the three most important bases on which air and bus travel can be compared or contrasted are the following:

1. speed
2. comfort
3. expense

Of course, there are many other bases on which air and bus travel might be compared or contrasted. In revising the paragraph above, for instance, the writer considered saying that while bus travel offers the opportunity to see the country, air travel offers sightseeing of another type—"skyseeing." He decided, however, that to discuss this would overburden a paragraph that must already deal with the three most important aspects of travel listed above. In revising, he contrasted air and bus travel only on those three bases, and the following paragraph was the result:

> If one can afford it, air travel offers several advantages over bus travel. Time is an important factor to consider. There is no such thing as nonstop traveling when one rides a bus for any considerable distance. It may take the traveler all day to travel across just one state. A bus stops

in every large city—and some buses stop at towns between the major cities—en route. In contrast, one can fly across the United States in a few short hours, saving precious time that can be used for business or pleasure. And because of the shortness of flying time, the passenger arrives more relaxed than after a long journey by bus. Comfort is another factor to consider. Although bus travel is more comfortable than it used to be, it still is not as comfortable as flying. Buses are frequently crowded and the ride can be bumpy. Air travel, on the other hand, is usually so smooth that one can easily sleep while flying. Also, in flight, attendants serve cold or hot drinks and meals; neither drinks nor food is served on buses. Of course, when it comes to price, one must pay for the comforts and speed of air travel, which is much more expensive than travel by bus. But for most people who travel long distances, the higher price is worth it.

Here the writer considers the two forms of travel with regard to speed, comfort, and expense and suggests that air travel is quicker and more comfortable than bus travel and worth the extra expense.

Two Ways to Organize and Present Your Material. There are two methods that are commonly used for organizing and presenting material in a formal comparison or contrast. The best way to understand these procedures is to set up a paragraph first by one arrangement and then by the other.

Suppose that you have been asked to write a paragraph comparing or contrasting two cars with four-wheel drive. First you must select two items that might be usefully compared or contrasted from the class "cars with four-wheel drive"—say the Chevrolet Blazer and the American Motors Jeep. Having compared and contrasted these cars in your mind, you might decide that it is important to focus on the differences between them because each car has its own advantages. Your paragraph, therefore, will contrast the two cars.

Next, you must go back over the various bases on which the two cars might be contrasted and select the most useful. You might decide that the following three are the most worthy of attention:

1. gas mileage
2. size
3. interior design

You are now ready to set up an outline and work up a plan for a good paragraph using one of the two methods of organizing a formal contrast. With the first method, you can make the two items being contrasted—the Blazer and the Jeep—the main entries in your outline and consider the bases under these headings, as in the following outline:

I. Topic Sentence
- A. Chevrolet Blazer
  1. Gas mileage
  2. Size
  3. Interior design
- B. American Motors Jeep
  1. Gas mileage
  2. Size
  3. Interior design

Alternatively, according to the second method, you can establish the three bases of contrast as main headings and then consider how each car measures up under each heading:

I. Topic Sentence
- A. Gas mileage
  1. The Blazer
  2. The Jeep
- B. Size
  1. The Blazer
  2. The Jeep
- C. Interior design
  1. The Blazer
  2. The Jeep

Experienced writers generally agree that the second method of organizing material is usually better. If you adopt the first method, you run the risk of writing at length on the Blazer and in the process making points which readers may forget when they reach the material on the Jeep. The contrast, therefore, may not be completely successful. On the other hand, if you follow the second method and take up each basis of contrast in turn, immediately treating first one car and then the other, the contrast may be sharper and more effective. In a brief paragraph, however, either method can work well.

Informal Comparison and Contrast

An informal comparison or contrast, like an informal definition, is not bound by strict rules. A comparison or contrast of two or more items must take place, but the rule that the items must be in the same class is not treated rigidly. In fact, the items under consideration may be placed in a class so large or so indefinite that it does not narrow or limit the discussion significantly. An airplane may be compared to an eagle, for instance, and the two may be said to belong to the broad class "objects that fly." This class would be too large to focus and limit a formal comparison. However, a writer who desires to show the power and grace of an airplane may compare it informally to an eagle in order to create a sharp image of strong and graceful flight.

Informal comparison or contrast is sometimes used to clarify an idea which might be harder to explain by another method of paragraph development. In the following paragraph, a student writer effectively uses informal comparison to express her attitudes toward television:

> My television set reminds me of a story I once read. A man found the most beautiful egg he had ever seen. The shell was very unusual because it looked like a piece of the rainbow. It seemed to glow with secret promises of wealth and fortune. The man took the egg home with him, and he polished it until it shone like glass. He placed it near the fire in his front room. Early the next morning the egg began to hatch. Soon there was an ugly monster standing in his front room. The man still tried to love it, but it turned on him and drove him from his home. Television is like that monster. Americans welcomed it into their homes and placed it at the heart of their lives. They idolized the stars who marched across the TV screen. Only recently have Americans realized that they have innocently harbored a monster. Hour after hour the television spits out nonsense like "White teeth for more sex appeal" or "You can be sure with SURE." The monster blinks at us unceasingly. It has hypnotized our children. Youngsters try to copy every move their TV idols make, and those moves are not always in the children's best interest. You can argue all day, but you will never convince a child that R-O-L-A-I-D-S doesn't spell "relief." So involved are our children with the fiend television that they can't do their homework until they have seen the latest episode of "The Incredible Hulk."

It is safe to say that the informal method of expressing feelings used in this paragraph is much more effective than a straightforward statement of complaints about television would be. Here the writer has taken a class—the class "monsters"—and stretched it imaginatively to cover an item which, strictly speaking, does not belong to the class at all. For the moment, the television set becomes a monster, and the writer's point is made strikingly and effectively.

SUMMARY

1. Use comparison to consider the likenesses between two items.
2. Use contrast to consider the differences between two items.
3. In formal comparison or contrast, consider items that are in the same class, and make sure that the class is sufficiently narrow for the comparison or contrast to be meaningful.

4. In formal comparison or contrast, select definite bases on which to rest a comparison or contrast, and restrict yourself to these bases in writing your paragraph.

5. In a paragraph developed by formal comparison or contrast, you may use either the items under consideration or the bases as main headings in outlining your paragraph. Usually the latter is preferable.

6. In informal comparison or contrast, you may relax the rules for formal comparison or contrast in order to support the controlling idea in a more effective way than formal comparison or contrast would allow.

7. In informal comparison or contrast, you may place one or both items under consideration in a very broad or even an imaginary or "farfetched" class.

EXERCISES

I. Analyze each of the following topic sentences carefully. Which sentences invite development by formal comparison or contrast? If formal comparison or contrast is indicated, in what class would the two terms be placed? What basis or bases would you use to rest a comparison or contrast on? If informal comparison or contrast is indicated, what broad or imaginary class might you employ?

    A. There are many fascinating similarities between Greek mythology and the stories in the Old Testament.

    B. Ice skating is more dangerous than roller skating.

    C. Students with good study habits earn higher grades than students with poor study habits.

    D. American football is a derivative of rugby.

informal   **E.** Life is often likened to a voyage.

II. Carefully read all of the following paragraphs. Then select three paragraphs and answer the questions about each:

    1. Is the paragraph developed by comparison or by contrast?

    2. Is the comparison or contrast formal or informal?

    3. If formal comparison or contrast is used, what are the bases for the comparison or contrast? Are the bases clear? Does the writer develop them fully?

    4. If informal comparison or contrast is used, what is the "class" into which the terms being compared or contrasted are placed?

In each case, explain whether or not the paragraph is effective. If the paragraph is poorly developed, explain ways in which it could be improved.

[handwritten margin note: doesn't compare]

A. Although electric and manual typewriters are used for the same purpose, there are several differences between the two machines. Electric typewriters are more expensive than manual typewriters. Prices for an electric typewriter begin at about $200. Electric typewriters are easy to use. No matter how irregular the typist's touch may be, electric typewriters turn out line after line of clear, sharp letters. Manual typewriters can be carried to places where there are no electrical outlets and can be used just about anywhere. Manual typewriters come in many colors, not just black or gray. Both manual and electric typewriters can be bought in business supply stores. Both manual and electric portable typewriters come in handy cases for easy carrying. For all-around use, such cases are hard to beat.

[handwritten margin note: compares but no conclusion]

B. Kung fu, the Chinese form of self-defense fighting, differs considerably from the modern Japanese version, known as karate. "Karate is straight line action," say some kung fu instructors, "while kung fu involves circular motions." Kung fu uses punches and kicks similar to those in karate, but kung fu movements are more flowing. A karate session looks like an army drill; a kung fu practice resembles a ballet. Karate fighters generally stand in one position and step forward or backward, while kung fu fighters move sideways and back and forth continually. Clawing and scratching are important in karate. Karate is easier to learn because the fighter remains relatively stationary, moving only the arms and legs. The kung fu fighter, on the other hand, is always moving and therefore needs to develop a high degree of coordination.

[handwritten margin note: bad]

C. To an inexperienced person, a hunting rifle and a target rifle may look alike, but to an experienced shooter, the differences are readily apparent. The mechanical build of each of these guns sets it apart from the other. The hunting rifle, which is often carried for long distances, is reasonably light. A target rifle, on the other hand, can weigh up to twice as much as a hunting rifle, since portability is not among the considerations that influence its design. The target rifle is delicate and must be protected from dust and moisture. Sights on a target rifle are often quite elaborate. If steel sights are used, they are usually intricate peep sights. The wide variety of scopes found on target rifles ranges up to 20 or 24 power. Those on hunting rifles range from 1.5 to 12 power.

D. People sometimes ask why they should buy a handmade Persian carpet when they can get a machine-made carpet that is just as attractive and costs less money. The answer is very simple. First, the materials used in a Persian carpet are gathered, selected, and treated by hand, and only the finest materials are used. Machine-made carpets, on the other hand, are made by inanimate devices that have no sense of quality and no ability to distinguish good materials from poor ones. Second, each handmade Persian carpet is unique; no other carpet is exactly like it. There is nothing unique, however, about a machine-made carpet. Hundreds and hundreds of identical carpets are produced by machines. Finally, the value of a Persian carpet increases with age, while a machine-made carpet is usually worthless after only a few years' use. As a result, machine-made carpets often wind up in the trash, while Persian carpets may turn up in museums. In short, each handmade Persian carpet is a work of art, and for this reason Persian carpets are much more valuable than their machine-made imitations.

E. Prejudice works like a slow poison after it has seeped into a human being. Like poison, it usually enters without the victim's knowledge. Poison and prejudice can enter the mind or spirit and spread to do their dark work. The person who is affected by prejudice is, unlike the recipient of poison, rarely aware of his ailment and does nothing to counteract the sinister agent. Just as slow-acting poison cripples the body, prejudice warps the human mind and spirit, and frequently distorts the victim's thoughts and actions. Unlike poison, prejudice does not kill its victim, but its effects are insidious and permanent unless the victim becomes aware of his condition and seeks an antidote.

F. For most Americans, breakfast is radically different from lunch and dinner: whereas most foods eaten at lunch can be served at dinner as well, breakfast foods are often reserved exclusively for the morning meal. Cereals, for example, are rarely served except at breakfast. The same is true for toast, which often appears on the breakfast table but rarely on the lunch or dinner table. In fact, part of the breakfast ritual in America involves browning bread to the desired shade and then buttering it. Bacon and eggs are a breakfast staple across the United States, but they are rarely served as a main dish at other meals. Jam and jelly appear most often at breakfast and only as an occasional extra at lunch and dinner. Unless one eats at an establishment which specializes in waffles and pancakes, these foods are usually consumed only

for breakfast. On the other hand, most items found on lunch
and dinner tables never show up at breakfast. Roasted meats
and fowls, for example, are hardly ever eaten for breakfast.
Salads and vegetables are likewise reserved almost exclusively for other meals. And those all-important dishes—soup
and dessert—which frequently begin and end lunch and
dinner just aren't to be found on American tables before
noon.

III. Write a paragraph on one of the following topics. Develop the
controlling idea by means of comparison or contrast. Employ either
a formal or informal approach. Before you start writing, be sure to
establish *definite bases* for any formal comparisons or contrasts that
you make.

A. attending a small college or attending a large university

B. two popular music groups

C. boots or shoes

D. two television advertisements

E. the good guys versus the bad guys

F. "Those were the days!"

G. college sports versus professional sports (you may choose
one particular sport to discuss)

IV. Write a paragraph on a topic of your own choosing. Develop
your paragraph by means of formal or informal comparison or contrast. If you use formal comparison or contrast, be certain that the
bases for your comparisons or contrasts are definite and clear.

Classification and Division

In paragraphs of formal classification or division, as in paragraphs of formal definition or of formal comparison or contrast, the
writer follows a set of established principles. It is also possible to relax
those principles and develop a paragraph by informal classification
or division. We will consider both approaches here.

Formal Classification

In developing a paragraph by comparison or contrast, the writer
evaluates objects and ideas by weighing their likenesses or differences. With classification and division, the writer examines an object
or an idea *by placing it into a broader class of which it is a part*
(classification) or *by dividing it into its basic parts* (division).

How formal classification and division work is illustrated in Figure 4–1, which shows the relationship of some of the members of the

Indo-European family of languages, which has more speakers than any other language family.

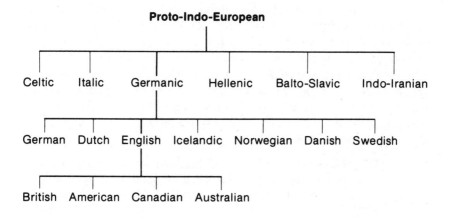

Proto-Indo-European

Figure 4-1

The chart shows languages that probably developed from a common ancestor, which we call *Proto-Indo-European* because the languages derived from it were spoken in an area that stretched from India across Europe. Four or five thousand years ago tribes of people speaking Proto-Indo-European began migrating from their homeland somewhere in northeastern Europe or western Asia. As the tribes spread into different parts of Europe and into India, the language spoken by each became increasingly unlike the languages spoken by other tribes. Slavic developed in eastern Europe, for example, while Germanic developed in northwestern Europe, and so on. In turn, people speaking these languages became further separated geographically, and over the centuries new linguistic subdivisions developed. As the chart shows, for instance, Germanic gradually became broken down into German, Dutch, English, and so forth. Furthermore, there are some differences in English as it is spoken today in Britain, the United States, Canada, and Australia.

   Figure 4-1 shows the relationship of the languages in a diagram of a *hierarchy,* or series of levels. In this hierarchy, an item on the lowest level belongs in the class of the next highest level; an item in this class, in turn, belongs in the class of the level above it; and so on until one reaches the highest, or all-inclusive level. According to the diagram we can say that English belongs to the more general class "Germanic"; thus we can *classify* English as a Germanic language. On the other hand, if we start at a high point in the hierarchy, say at the level of "Germanic," we can *divide* that class into seven parts:

German, Dutch, English, Icelandic, Norwegian, Danish, and Swedish. English, in turn, can be divided into the varieties spoken in Britain, the United States, and so on.

In writing a paragraph developed by formal classification or division, you should remember that *whether you classify or divide depends on the point from which you look at your subject*—that is, on your perspective. When you *classify,* you are working *upward* in a hierarchy; when you *divide,* you are working *downward.* In paragraphs of classification or division, *your topic sentence indicates your perspective and commits you to either classifying or dividing.* A paragraph developed by *classification,* for example, might have the following topic sentence:

> The millions of people who speak English may be grouped into four large classes: those speaking British English, those speaking American English, those speaking Australian English, and those speaking Canadian English.

Here you start on the level of the millions of individual speakers of English and *classify* them—that is, place them in the appropriate category—according to the dialect they speak. A paragraph developed by division, on the other hand, might have the following topic sentence:

> The English language has four major dialects: British English, American English, Canadian English, and Australian English.

In a paragraph with this topic sentence, the writer starts with the general subject "English," rather than with individual speakers of English, and divides the language according to the major dialects which make it up.

There are two rules to remember in developing a paragraph by formal classification or division:

1. Select a basis or bases for classification or division and formulate those bases precisely before you begin writing.
2. When you are classifying or dividing, your categories must be mutually exclusive; if one item fits into more than one category, your categories are faulty.

Selecting Precise Bases for Classification or Division. In a paragraph developed by classification or division, *you must be sure that the bases on which you classify or divide are suitably precise* and that you do not stray from them. Without clear bases for classification or division, your paragraph is likely to become muddled. Consider the following paragraph in which a student attempts to *divide* the student body of Pinkerton College:

The student body of Pinkerton College is highly varied. Although most of the students are from North America, many are also from Europe and Asia. Some are from South America, and others from France and Germany. Pinkerton is especially noted for its musicology department, and some of the college's best students are musicology majors. Some of the musicology students are also interested in languages or fine arts. There are also students in the colleges of Liberal Arts, Business Administration, and Education. There are many English majors. Pinkerton offers a wide choice of majors for its students.

In this paragraph, the bases on which the writer divides the subject "student body" are not at all clear. He begins by dividing the subject according to *place of origin;* he has apparently not decided, though, whether place of origin should be specified in terms of continents (North America, Europe, and so on) or countries (France and Germany). The precise basis for division should have been either *continental origin* or *national origin,* and the writer should have used one or the other consistently. The writer apparently also tries to divide "student body" according to the *academic major* selected by each student, but the students are sometimes said to be majoring in a *College* (for example, the College of Liberal Arts), and sometimes in a *subject* (for example, English). Again the precise bases for division are unclear.

Selecting Mutually Exclusive Categories. When classifying or dividing, always choose categories that are mutually exclusive and do not overlap one another. This rule is violated in the preceding paragraph. The students' places of origin are identified as North America, Europe, Asia, South America, France, and Germany. The overlap occurs because France and Germany are *parts* of the broader category "Europe." By listing them separately the writer is in effect counting French and German students twice. There is also an overlap in the division according to *academic majors.* Students with an English major are listed separately, even though they have already been included in the larger category of students in the College of Liberal Arts. Thus the divisions in this paragraph are muddled and leave the reader with imprecise information.

The paragraph might be more effectively written as follows:

Students at Pinkerton College have varying backgrounds and academic interests: they come from different parts of the world, and they are interested in different fields of academic specialization. Although most of the students are from North America, many are from South America, some are from Europe, and a few are from Asia. Pinkerton is especially noted for its musicology department, which draws many majors each year. It also graduates a large number of majors in English, business administration, chemistry, and education. The student who attends Pinkerton will be among students of widely differing backgrounds and with widely differing academic interests.

In this paragraph, the student body is divided on the basis of *continental point of origin* and on the basis of *major subject*. There is no overlapping in the divisions, and the paragraph is successful.

Informal Classification or Division

A paragraph can also be developed by *informal* classification or division. A writer using this method still establishes precise bases on which to classify or divide but relaxes or ignores the rule against overlap. Furthermore, the classes of items he deals with are often set up in accord with the purely personal perspective of the writer. Consider, for example, the following paragraph:

> I have had many types of teachers in my fourteen years as a student, but the instructors I remember best were the intellectuals, good guys, and teachers I had crushes on. The intellectuals weren't too strict, but they were always demanding. They demanded my time, my efforts, and my brains and would, on occasion, reward me with an "A"—if I was lucky. Good guys were usually coaches who taught courses like "Popular Culture" or "National Problems" to supplement their income. Good guys would let you sleep in class if they thought you were tired. And they wouldn't get on you if you were unprepared. Finally, there were the teachers I had crushes on. They were all, to my way of thinking, either handsome or cute. They could be intellectuals or good guys, but if I liked them, I didn't care. I did my best work for them outside of class and spent time in class daydreaming about them and their private lives. Were they married? Did they have kids? Did they wear blue jeans when they weren't teaching school? Of course, I had other teachers. Dummies, idiots, and phonies were a few I encountered, not to mention frustrated comedians, frustrated actors, and those who were just plain frustrated. But the ones I remember best are the ones who asked a great deal of me, the ones who asked only that I come to class, and the ones I hung my fantasies on.

This paragraph classifies teachers from the *personal* viewpoint of one student. There is nothing scientific about the classification. The writer puts the teachers she remembers best into three classes which are meaningful to her personally. And her classification does not observe the rule against double listing, or overlap, because the third category (teachers she had crushes on) can also include some members of the first category (teachers who were intellectuals) and the second (teachers who were good guys). The result is an interesting and well-written paragraph developed by informal classification.

A Word of Caution: Avoiding Oversimplification

In writing a paragraph developed by classification or division, avoid simplistic assertions that there are three categories of a given item: the one extreme, the opposite extreme, and the in-between. A paragraph, for example, that classifies students into three categories —"those who study hard and never go to parties," "those who scarcely study at all and spend a great deal of time socializing," and "those who balance the time they spend studying and socializing"— is not likely to be very effective. Such a classification is too pat. It overlooks many other kinds of students. There is nothing wrong, of course, with writing a three-class or three-division paragraph—provided that the three categories you include reflect your subject accurately or, as in informal classification and division, deal with it originally.

SUMMARY

1. Developing a paragraph by classification or division involves examining something by dividing it into its basic parts (division) or by showing how it fits into a broader class of which it is a part (classification).
2. Whether you classify or divide depends on the point from which you look at your subject—that is, on your perspective.
3. When you classify, you are working upward in a hierarchy or series of levels. You are putting the item into a class that is at a higher level in the hierarchy.
4. When you divide, you are working downward in a hierarchy. You are dividing the subject into smaller parts that make it up—that is, into parts of the hierarchic level immediately under it.
5. In paragraphs of classification or division, your topic sentence indicates your perspective and commits you to either classifying or dividing.
6. In formal classification or division, you must establish precise bases on which to rest the classification or division.
7. In formal classification or division, you must be sure that no item falls into more than one class or division. In other words, make certain that classes or divisions are mutually exclusive.
8. In informal classification or division, your point of view may be personal. Classes or divisions still must have precise bases, but the rule against overlap may be relaxed or, occasionally, ignored.

EXERCISES

I. Consider each of the following topic sentences carefully. Is the topic sentence one which lends itself to development by means of classification or division? Which method would you use? Why? What precise bases for classifying or dividing would you use? Could the idea contained in the sentence be developed effectively by informal classification or division? If so, how would you go about doing it?

A. There are many different kinds of holidays.

B. Automobile drivers fall into several basic categories.

C. Athletes are either "amateurs" or "professionals."

D. There are several ways to classify dogs.

E. The average citizen is exposed to advertising from television, radio, magazines, and newspapers.

F. Any checker at a supermarket can tell you that every shopper falls into one of several categories.

II. In each of the paragraphs below, a student writer has attempted development by classification or division. Read each paragraph carefully, and answer the following questions:

1. Does the writer employ classification or division?

2. Is the method formal or informal?

3. If the method is formal, what are the bases for classification or division?

4. Is there any overlap in categorizing the items?

5. Is the paragraph successful? Why, or why not?

6. If the method employed is informal, in what way are the rules for formal classification or division relaxed? What does the writer gain by using informal classification or division?

A. Carnivorous plants, which are distinguished from other plants by virtue of their ability to entrap and digest unwary insects, can be divided into two groups according to the way in which they catch their prey: active trappers and passive trappers. The familiar Venus's flytrap belongs in the class of the active trappers. The leaf structure of the flytrap contains tactile trigger hairs which protrude from a convex hinged surface. When an unsuspecting insect touches one or more of these hairs, the leaf closes, and the insect is trapped inside. Once the leaf is closed, glands on the surface of the leaf secrete enzymes which digest the entrapped victim and thereby supply nutrients to the plant. The equally well-known pitcher plant fits into the category of the passive trappers. This plant exudes an enticing nectar which lures insects into a slippery funnel containing a reservoir of digestive fluid. The fluid then digests the trapped insect, turning it into a form of nutrition which can be utilized as food for the plant. Carnivorous plants like the Venus's flytrap and the pitcher plant possess unique and subtle skills, and they must be considered one of nature's more exotic experiments.

B. The fabrics and colors of costumes worn by actors during Shakespeare's time were highly symbolic. Commoners wore coarse gray wool. Working men usually wore rough canvas aprons. Servants were always seen in tawny blue clothing. Fools dressed in several colors, of which yellow was usually the most prominent. Members of the nobility dressed in satin, taffeta, damask, or velvet. The queen often appeared in costumes made from scarlet or purple material. Sometimes she even appeared in a calico dress. Because calico was imported from India and hence enormously expensive, only a queen could afford to wear a calico outfit.

C. There are, of course, as many individual reasons for failing to vote as there are people who don't vote, but these reasons tend to fall into several categories. Unnecessarily strict voting laws often keep many people from voting. Poll tax laws and "grandfather" clauses are among the types of legislation which discriminate against voters by making it difficult for them to vote. Many college students who attend out-of-state schools cannot vote in the state where their schools are located. Other people fail to vote because they lack interest in either of the major political parties. Many of today's voters feel less and less committed to a specific party, and as a result they don't feel an allegiance to a team and have little personal motivation to vote. The largest group of stay-at-home eligible voters, however, is probably made up of people who simply have a feeling that they, as individual citizens, have little effect on the outcome of elections. These voters feel powerless and thus alienated. Apathy toward voting is the outcome, and recent scandals involving high-ranking public officials have contributed greatly to this apathy. In conclusion, it is safe to say that most people who don't vote are either prevented by law from voting, are apathetic to both political parties, or just feel that their votes don't count.

D. There are three major misconceptions concerning the Crusades. First, many people think that the Crusades were successful. In reality, however, they were not. Although the

Christian nobles who led the Crusades achieved their goal of taking Jerusalem from the Muslims, a little more than a century later the Muslims regained control of the city. Second, many people believe that the Christian nobles who participated in the Crusades followed the codes of chivalry. In reality, however, these nobles were anything but chivalrous. On one occasion, for instance, they sacked Constantinople, a city they were supposed to protect. Most of the nobles who went on the Crusades were opportunists. They hoped that the Crusades would make them rich, and they took every opportunity, chivalrous or otherwise, to make themselves rich. In many instances, the Crusades were merely an excuse Christian knights used to plunder and pillage. Some knights even became kings of captured territory in the Holy Land. Third, many people assume that the Crusades initiated an exchange of culture and learning between the East and the West. Actually, however, there was little exchange between Muslim and Christian cultures. Muslims were highly literate and communicated primarily through the written word. Christian nobles, most of whom believed that reading and writing were below their dignity, learned little from the Muslims, and vice versa.

E. There are several ways in which car owners can prevent burglaries and can help to ensure the return of their cars in the event that a theft does take place. First, car owners can take precautions which make theft difficult. The most obvious is locking a car, even one left for a short time in a safe parking lot. At night, drivers should park in well-lighted areas only. They should be sure never to leave the keys in the car, even for a few moments. The owner who parks overnight in the driveway can prevent theft by parking with the front of the car facing the street, so that a prospective car thief will run the risk of being seen tampering with the engine. Second, when buying a new car, a driver should insist on having the new devices which have been developed to discourage theft, such as tapered door locks and an alarm system. Third, the car owner can take measures which ensure against the theft of items from the car. Here, again, locking the car helps. Packages, clothing, luggage, and sports equipment should be locked in the trunk, not left on the seat in plain view. Finally, car owners can take precautions which will help the police to identify a car if it is stolen. They can remove license and registration cards from the car when it is not in use, thus making it difficult for thieves to sell the car. All car owners should know the identification numbers on their cars, and they can even mark the car somewhere out of sight with a mark known to no one else. They can also place a small card with a name on it somewhere inside a seat. Identification numbers and hidden markings facilitate the location and return of stolen motor vehicles.

III. Write a paragraph on one of the topics listed below. Develop the paragraph by use of formal classification or formal division. Be sure that you establish bases on which to rest your classification or division, and be sure that no item in your classification or division falls into more than one category. When you have finished this paragraph, select another topic and write a paragraph using informal classification or division as your method of development. You may use the same topic for both a formal and an informal paragraph.

    A. junk food

    B. popular music

    C. thieves

    D. suckers

    E. heroes

    F. patriots

    G. football fans

    H. villains

IV. Write a paragraph on a topic of your own choosing. Develop your paragraph by means of classification or division. If you use formal classification or formal division, be sure that you rest your classification or division on precise bases, and make certain that your bases don't overlap.

Cause and Effect

One of the most frequently used methods of development in contemporary writing is *cause and effect*. Its frequent use is perfectly natural in this scientific age. As a result of the scientific approach to understanding the world and our experiences in it, we have come to assume that there is a cause (or causes) for every event and that, conversely, every event has results or effects.

Like comparison and contrast, cause and effect may be said to constitute two sides of the same coin. If you can develop a paragraph using cause, you should have no trouble developing a paragraph using effect—the techniques involved in each approach are the same. And like comparison and contrast, cause and effect are means of communicating relationships. The kinds of relationships they deal with are different, however. In using comparison and contrast, you examined two people, things, ideas, or events *side by side*, so to speak, and looked for their likenesses or differences. Now, in using cause and effect, you examine an event in relation to other events that *precede* or *follow* it. In other words, you show *why* an event has occurred by examining its causes, or you show what happens *as a result of* the event by examining its effects.

There are two rules to follow if you want to use cause and effect competently:

1. Cite the most important and convincing causes or effects. This means looking for causes or effects that are clearly and directly related to the event under consideration.
2. Be sure that in using cause and effect you do not mistake mere conditions or circumstances for active causes or effects.

Citing Important and Convincing Causes and Effects. In developing a paragraph by cause and effect, you must be sure that what you label "effect" clearly and directly resulted from what you label "cause." In other words, you must be convincing and accurate when you say that A was the cause or the effect of B.

In the following student paragraph, developed by an examination of cause, the writer does not accomplish this successfully:

> The intersection of Geyer Springs Road and Interstate 30 causes more automobile accidents than does any other intersection in Little Rock. It has been reported that thousands of cars pass through the intersection every day. This statistic should signal to motorists that they ought to be careful when driving in this heavily congested area. But improper driving habits often prevail. Very often one hears the screech of brakes as one driver pulls out in front of another. Careless driving causes accidents because one driver may swerve out of a lane to keep from hitting the car ahead, only to find his or her car smashing into the side of the car in the lane alongside. Drivers should also be careful about tuning in favorite radio programs at this intersection. And parents should never talk to children in the back seat of the car when driving through this dangerous intersection. Lack of concentration can result in accidents in any lane of this busy location.

This paragraph is obviously muddled. The writer starts out with the assumption that, because more traffic accidents have occurred at the intersection of Geyer Springs Road and Interstate 30 than at any other intersection in Little Rock, the intersection is therefore the *cause* of the high accident rate. While the intersection may in fact be more hazardous than any other in the city (it may be busier, or located near a blind curve, or whatever), the writer has provided no evidence to support such a claim. Furthermore, most accidents are caused by careless or inexperienced drivers. The writer apparently is aware of this since most of her paragraph deals with driving habits. She might, therefore, have written a more convincing paragraph if she had organized her ideas around the following topic sentence:

> The junction of Geyer Springs Road and Interstate 30 is hazardous, and the carelessness of drivers entering this intersection has resulted in its having become the scene of more accidents than any other intersection in Little Rock.

The student paragraph that follows illustrates a convincing treatment of causal forces at work:

> A series of events led to the collapse of Elvis Presley's career. His wife, Priscilla, moved out of Graceland Mansion in 1972, leaving Elvis depressed and alone. Immediately after Priscilla left, Elvis's buddies moved in and involved the rock star in a series of round-the-clock parties. As a result of overindulgence in party fare and failure to exercise, Elvis found himself with a serious weight problem. By 1974 he weighed 240 pounds and was so fat that when he appeared in Las Vegas, photographers were forbidden to take pictures of him. A crash diet, which was supposed to reduce the singer's weight, instead brought on a prolonged period of depression from which he never really recovered. Appalled at his heaviness, audiences rejected the overweight entertainer, and his career rapidly deteriorated.

After finishing this paragraph, the reader feels that the writer has pointed out some valid causes of the collapse of Elvis Presley's career. The analysis proceeds through a series of events, beginning with the separation of the singing star and his wife and ending with the decline of Elvis's popularity. Each event in the series is *believably attributed to a cause,* and the final outcome is the deterioration of Presley's career—the occurrence the paragraph set out to explain.

In a paragraph developed by cause or effect, the writer must describe the causes or effects in such a way that the reader is convinced of their direct relationship to the event being discussed. The following paragraph, which describes the effects of television commercials on the writer, accomplishes this very well:

> Television commercials certainly have an effect on me, but I don't suppose that the effect they have would delight the advertisers who spend their days concocting such pabulum for the "tube." When a commercial or series of commercials comes on television, I sometimes turn the sound on the set down and pick up a book or a magazine to read until the program resumes. Often I leave the room for a few minutes. Getting a snack, doing a bit of cooking, or even going to the

bathroom are activities far superior to pondering the virtue of "X" brand of soap or worrying about whether my oven is clean enough for Aunt Matilda's inspection. Television commercials lack what I think I've got: native intelligence. The result is that I feel intellectually insulted and psychologically abused by commercials when I know that neither the commercials nor many of the products they promote are any boon to our existence. And that native intelligence in me, that sixth sense which screams out about my rights being violated, frequently causes me to reach out my hand at those unfortunate times when commercial slots loom and to turn the volume down, down, off.

Mistaking Conditions or Circumstances for Active Causes or Effects. Very often, through faulty reasoning, people assume that a state of affairs or an event causes another event, when in fact the so-called "cause" is not directly responsible at all. They mistake circumstances for actual causes.

In the following paragraph, for example, environmental circumstances are confused with *causes:*

> An attractive environment causes children to become emotionally stable and productive. Because of the comfortable setting, they feel confident and trusting of themselves and others. They are happier, make more friends, and enjoy school activities more. Children even earn higher grades when they study in attractive surroundings. Their parents may be happier in an attractive home, and if so the children are happier because they know that their mother and father are contented. It is amazing how much better children function when they live in a beautiful and attractive environment.

An attractive environment does not *cause* a child to become emotionally stable and productive. It provides a setting which may allow a state of well-being to develop, but it does not necessarily bring about emotional development of any kind. We all know of children who live in beautiful homes but who are unhappy because their parents are divorced, because there is serious illness in the family, or because they are neglected by busy or uncaring parents.

SUMMARY

1. Cause and effect is a frequently used method of paragraph development because, in the scientific world in which we live, we are accustomed to thinking in terms of causes and effects.
2. Use cause and effect when you want to show *why* an event has occurred (by examining its causes) or when you want to show what happens *as a result of* the event (by examining its effects).
3. Be sure that you cite important causes and effects and that you present them convincingly.

4. Be sure that you deal with causes or effects that are clearly and directly related to the event under consideration.

5. Do not mistake mere circumstances for active causes or effects.

EXERCISES

I. Following are seven topic sentences which may be developed by the use of cause and effect. Read each sentence and state whether it would be developed more effectively in a paragraph of cause or a paragraph of effect. List the causes or the effects which should be included in developing and supporting the topic sentence.

  A. For a long time, humans have been carelessly polluting the planet on which they live.

  B. The new student union has become an important part of student life at River City College.

  C. Grades sometimes fail to show what a student learns.

  D. Disco music has changed the lives of America's young people.

  E. Watching television has ill effects on many children.

  F. Color affects one's moods.

  G. People lie for a variety of reasons.

II. Carefully read all of the following paragraphs. Each shows a student's attempt to develop a paragraph by cause or effect. Some paragraphs use the method well; others are not so effective. After considering each paragraph, answer the following questions:

  1. Has the writer of the paragraph attempted to develop it by cause or by effect?

  2. Is the attempt successful or not? Give explicit reasons for your answer.

  3. Which paragraphs, if any, merely show *circumstances* conducive to producing a result rather than actual *causes* of the result?

  A. There are many situations which cause pressure and tension to build up inside of us. Performing in front of an audience commonly produces pressure. We suffer from fear of making an embarrassing mistake during the performance. Many of us also experience tension when we are among new people. In such situations, we become quiet out of fear that other people will label us as "loud mouths." Coaches and athletes often feel tension before big games because they do not want to commit errors that might cause their teams to lose. I feel tension right now as I write this paragraph. I want it to be the best paragraph I've written this semester, for I know that this is my last chance to better my grade in this course. Pressure and tension are common in our environment. No matter how hard we try to avoid them, there will inevitably be times when breathing becomes hard and fear gets a grip on us that is difficult to loosen.

B. In the past few years, higher education has become increasingly important to young people everywhere. Higher education is essential for those who wish to enter the fields of medicine, engineering, and communications. These fields are essential for the survival of the human race. In the future, successful people will undoubtedly be those who have received technical instruction in fields such as these. Without this education, mankind cannot survive. The very existence of the human race depends on man's ability to progress in highly technical fields.

C. Entering a hospital isn't always in one's best interest. Many doctors give a standard battery of tests to every incoming patient. Such a procedure means that some patients receive more tests than they actually need. Sometimes these tests can even be dangerous. X-rays, for example, involve radiation, and exposure to radiation can sometimes result in birth deformities or in cancer. Before many medical tests, the patient must undergo enemas which involve the use of harsh laxatives that sometimes dehydrate the body. Most doctors feel that individually these tests do little harm to a patient; however, doctors don't seem to take into consideration the fact that the average hospital patient may receive as many as four or five tests in a single day. This many tests can weaken even a healthy person. In addition, statistics indicate that 9 percent of all hospital patients contract an illness or infection while in the hospital. So sometimes the cure is worse than the disease.

D. Today's children are rapidly losing respect for their parents. The principal cause of this phenomenon is lack of leadership on the part of parents. Too frequently the answer to the question, "Who's the boss, Mom or Dad?" is an unhelpful "Neither!" Unlike the fathers of the past, today's dads lack authority. One father summarized the problem this way: "Whatever Grandfather did was done with authority; whatever we do is done with hesitation." Mom is also to blame. Afraid that she may lose her children's love, she denies them nothing. Another reason that children are losing respect for their parents is parental failure to provide guidelines for the behavior of their children. Children need guidelines. They need and want clear definitions of acceptable and unacceptable social behavior. Despite this need, parents stand back uncertainly and let their children make the rules. Children don't respect elders who seem unable to lay down guidelines for how to behave. Finally, lack of discipline generates disrespect among children. When they misbehave, children need discipline. Too often today's parents administer discipline, if at all, in a haphazard and unsystematic fashion, lashing out at their children with harsh words, quick slaps, or strange denials which children don't understand. Random discipline confuses children. Often they don't see any logic to its application or timing.

E. One reason to take up jogging is the company. If you have friends who jog, for instance, you may naturally start to jog yourself. When you jog with others, the time passes more quickly, and you do not feel conspicuous when people stare at you because you know that you are one of a group. Jogging along with others enables you to measure your endurance by comparing it to the stamina of your companions. In addition, if you jog in the morning, you can stop for a cup of coffee afterwards while in the company of one or two of your fellow runners. Friendship is a major reason why Americans devote so much energy to jogging.

III. Using cause or effect, develop a paragraph on one of the following topics. Decide whether the topic can be better developed by dealing with causes or by dealing with effects, and then formulate your topic sentence so that the purpose of the paragraph is clear. Be careful not to confuse circumstances with actual causes.

   A. collecting antiques (or stamps or anything else that people commonly collect)

   B. censorship

   C. suicide

   D. discrimination

   E. advertising

   F. hunting

   G. dieting

   H. adult education

IV. Using cause or effect as your method of development, write a paragraph on a topic of your own choosing. Be sure that you cite causes and effects that are important and directly related and that you do not mistake circumstances for active causes or effects.

Process Analysis

Like cause and effect, *process analysis,* the sixth method of development, is particularly important in our science-oriented society. Much of what we do—from assembling a model airplane to attending a political convention—requires an understanding of how things work. And much of what we observe—from how a vegetable garden grows to how Congress passes a law—arouses our interest in how things come about. Process analysis is a method of communicating such information.

Process analysis has a wide variety of uses. Instructions, for example, are usually a form of process analysis. Directions for assembling a model airplane describe a process to be followed to obtain a desired result. A recipe containing instructions for making a lemon pie describes a process, as do instructions for developing film. A slightly different use of process analysis is seen in accounts of biological processes—how leaves change color, for example, or how a caterpillar develops into a butterfly. Process analysis might also be used to describe the standard process that students go through when they register for classes at the beginning of each semester. We read of mechanical processes, biological processes, chemical processes, and processes established by human law or custom.

In developing a paragraph by process analysis, the writer is considering a series of steps, toward a specific end, which take place in a certain order. Thus, *all processes involve a series of events in time.* Further, in order to be a process, the series must be one which is, or can be, repeated. Thus, an account of a particular Civil War battle will reveal a series of events which necessarily occurred in time, but it cannot be called process analysis because no other battle would repeat that series of events.

In addition, it is important to note that you may write *about* a process, such as a school registration, but unless you treat the event *as a process*—as a series of events in time which can be repeated— you will not be using process analysis. Suppose that you do write a paragraph recounting the events of a long morning spent in registering for spring-term classes. If you treat the stages of the activity simply as events in your day, you won't be writing a process analysis; instead, you will be writing a narrative, or story, about this particular morning. But if your account of the event explains the series of steps you followed and which *every* student must follow at registration— from picking up the information kit to receiving a complete class-schedule card—then you will have developed your paragraph by process analysis.

The rules involved in developing a paragraph by process analysis are relatively simple. Basically, you must be sure that you present a series of steps that are either necessarily or customarily involved in bringing about a certain result and that you present all the steps, in the order in which they normally occur. In the following paragraph, the writer had intended to explain the process by which a campfire is built, but his explanation is incomplete because he did not list *all* the steps involved in the order in which they belong:

> Building a good campfire involves a routine which the serious camper learns very early. The camper must know what kind of wood to use and then must find some wood of this type. To start a fire, he needs three things: matches, dead grass, and twigs. Also desirable are some pine wood, for starting the fire, and some spruce wood, for keeping the fire going. The experienced camper takes care to add new wood to the fire stick by stick, for too many pieces added at one time may put the fire out or cause a lot of smoke. By following these steps, almost anyone can build a campfire successfully.

This paragraph gives a prospective camper helpful information about starting a campfire, but there are gaps that must be filled in for the reader to have a complete, step-by-step picture of the process. We are told, for example, that matches, dead grass, and twigs are needed to build a good campfire, but we are never told how to use these items. Moreover, the preliminary steps in the process—preparations for building a fire—are completely omitted.

The following revised paragraph is much more complete:

> Building a good campfire involves a routine which the serious camper learns very early. Before trying to start a fire, the camper prepares a site. He clears an area with a radius of about ten feet to ensure that the fire will not spread. He then gathers the following materials: dry grass, dry twigs, and some pine and spruce wood. In laying the fire, the camper first makes a small pile of grass in the center of the firesite. He then stacks twigs in a pyramidal or tepee shape around the grass. He usually starts the fire with matches, though the experienced camper can also start it by rubbing two sticks together if necessary. As the fire progresses, he adds small sticks of dry pine wood and then larger pieces as the fire spreads out and becomes hotter. When the fire is very hot and is thoroughly established, he adds spruce wood or another long-burning wood if such is available. He takes care to add new wood to the fire stick by stick, for too many pieces added at one time may put the fire out or cause a lot of smoke. By following these steps, almost anyone can build a campfire successfully.

This paragraph is carefully and properly developed. The writer has presented all the steps involved in starting a fire, in the order in which they should be taken. Readers can now understand the process of building a fire and can even repeat it if they wish.

SUMMARY

1. A process involves a number of events which are customarily repeated and which lead to a specific end.
2. In developing a paragraph through process analysis, the writer should include all the important steps that are either necessarily or customarily involved in the process.
3. The steps in the process should be presented in the order in which they necessarily or customarily occur.

EXERCISES

I. Read the following topic sentences carefully. Each sentence lends itself to development by process analysis. List the steps that are involved in the process to be described. Be sure that you do not omit any important steps. Then list the steps in the sequence in which they occur.

> **A.** Washing a car requires more thought than people may realize.
>
> **B.** Painting a room requires a good deal of planning.
>
> **C.** From being seated to giving a tip, getting a meal in a restaurant has become a ritual.
>
> **D.** Growers of houseplants should learn how to repot a plant correctly.
>
> **E.** Washing dishes is a set routine for millions of people.

II. Read each of the following paragraphs. Is the writer concerned with a process, or is the paragraph simply an account of a happening or a series of happenings? If a process is presented, has the author included all the steps in the process, or have some steps been omitted? Does the writer treat any factors which are not actually steps in the process?

> **A.** Some people can quit smoking as soon as they decide to stop, but for most people breaking the habit takes time and effort. When smokers decide to stop smoking, they must be determined to break the habit. At first, smokers should keep a careful record of the times when they most desire to smoke. They should also list the number of cigarettes they smoke each day and then reduce that number each day thereafter. Depending on their will power, they may give up those cigarettes which are most important to them or those which are least important. In any event, they will gradually begin to withdraw from the habit. During the process of with-

drawal, smokers should put cigarettes and matches where they cannot be reached without effort. Cigarettes should be put in one place and matches in another, so that smokers are forced to take several steps before satisfying their urge to smoke. Smokers should avoid activities which they formerly accompanied with a smoke. If determined to smoke, smokers should try to postpone lighting up a cigarette for fifteen minutes, then for thirty minutes, and then for longer periods. They should also keep a weekly record of the total number of cigarettes smoked and allot a smaller number of cigarettes for the week to follow. Smokers whose appetite for food increases to the point where they gain weight excessively should plan a careful schedule of exercise. Throughout the entire process, prospective nonsmokers should remember the pledge they once affirmed and hang on stubbornly to the determination which will carry them through.

B. Have you ever wondered why leaves turn color in the autumn? In late summer and early fall, a ring of corky cells grows across the base of the leaf, slowly blocking the routes which carry food and water to and from the blade. By early October, the vein system of the leaf is totally cut off from its former source of nourishment. Without water, the leaf stops making food. Green chlorophyll disappears, and a bright yellow pigment called xanthophyll, which during the summer had been masked by the green of the chlorophyll, gradually becomes visible. Leaves that contain a substance called carotene start to turn red or orange. Deep reds and purples show up in leaves which contain a chemical compound called anthocyanin. At last the transformation from summer to fall colors is complete. With its nourishment cut off, the leaf loses all its green and yellow coloring and bursts forth into a brilliant and dazzling display of beauty.

C. About a year and a half ago, when I was in one of my annual "It's time for a change" moods, I stopped eating meat. I have felt healthier and happier ever since. I had been reading with great interest about the pros and cons of low-protein diets when I began to entertain the possibility of becoming a vegetarian. At the time meat prices were soaring, as they still are, and the fact that I was living in a college dormitory and eating cafeteria food of unknown origin forced me to consider the possibility all the more seriously. To test my curiosity and will power, I eliminated all forms of beef from my diet and gradually cut back my consumption of poultry and pork. Realizing that I was losing weight and feeling better than I had in several years, I stopped eating meat altogether. Vegetables, fruits, and dairy products began to taste better, and I knew that I had successfully replaced an old habit with a new, healthier one.

D. To make good lasagna, follow these simple instructions. First, slowly brown one pound of Italian sausage and spoon off the excess grease. Stir in the following ingredients: one clove of minced garlic, one tablespoon chopped fresh basil, one and a half teaspoons salt, one one-pound can of tomatoes, and two six-ounce cans of tomato paste. Simmer the ingredients for thirty minutes, stirring occasionally. In the meantime, cook ten ounces of lasagna noodles in boiling salted water until tender, drain the water, and rinse the noodles. Next, beat two eggs and add three cups cream-style cottage cheese. Add to the egg mixture the following ingredients: one-half cup grated Parmesan cheese, two tablespoons parsley flakes, one teaspoon salt, and one-half teaspoon pepper. Next, assemble the four items to be layered: the noodles, the cottage cheese-egg mixture, one pound of mozzarella cheese, and the meat sauce. To layer, first place one-third of the noodles in a $13 \times 9 \times 2$-inch baking dish. Cover the noodles with some cottage cheese filling, add a layer of mozzarella cheese, and cover with meat sauce. Repeat this procedure twice until all the ingredients are used up. Bake the lasagna at 350° for about thirty minutes. When the lasagna is done, let it stand for about ten minutes before serving.

E. Saddling a horse is not as difficult as it may seem. First, place the saddle blanket high on the horse's shoulders; then slide it down to the middle of the back. This operation flattens the hair under the blanket and helps prevent the formation of painful galls. Next, pick the saddle up and fold the right stirrup over the seat to keep it from catching under the saddle. Then place the saddle gently on the horse's back. To settle it, shake the saddle carefully. Then reach under the horse's belly and pull the girth toward you. Tighten the girth gradually but firmly. If the girth is too tight, it may produce sores on the horse's flesh; if it is too loose, the saddle may fall off when the rider tries to mount. It should be just tight enough to allow the rider to slip two fingers between the girth and the horse's belly. Before trying to mount, grasp the saddle by the horn and pull. If the saddle stays firm and doesn't give, the horse is ready for a rider.

F. Waking up in the morning is a struggle between the mind

and the body. Usually the body arouses the sleeper into a state of semi-consciousness, which jolts the mind into thinking. The first thought which emerges is usually, "Oh my gosh, I am awake." The mind then tells the body to find a more comfortable position. This order usually backfires because the body doesn't know what position to assume. Tossing and turning, the body signals the mind that it is uncomfortable. This signal starts a chain reaction which eventually leads both the mind and the body to accept the fact that the time has come to get up. Then, for no apparent reason, the eyes open and stare across the room. The mind then thinks, "I have to get up"—a thought which causes the mind to panic and the body to rebel. At this time the mind decides that it doesn't want to get up, and the battle continues. Eventually the body reluctantly begins to get up, usually to the accompaniment of yawns, stretches, and itchy eyes. Within a few short minutes, the mind and the body are both awakened to the point of full consciousness, and the war is finally over.

III. Write a paragraph on one of the following topics. Develop your paragraph by means of process analysis. Be careful to explain each step in the process and to place it in the correct time sequence.

   A. changing a flat tire

   B. preparing for an exam

   C. washing dishes

   D. flying in an airplane for the first time

   E. writing a paragraph

   F. frying an egg (or making fudge, etc.)

   G. preparing to face the world each morning

IV. Using process analysis as your method of development, write a paragraph on a topic of your own choosing. Make sure that you include all the steps involved in the process being discussed and that you present the steps in the order in which they occur.

Using Methods of Development

Now that you have studied six of the methods available for developing general-to-specific expository paragraphs, you can put your knowledge of them to work for you in two ways:

   1. If you have been assigned a topic but are finding it hard to decide on a controlling idea for a paragraph, a consideration of the six methods may help you.

2. If you already have a controlling idea, a consideration of the six methods should help you to select the best method to use in developing your paragraph.

Deciding on a Controlling Idea

One of the important ways in which you can use your knowledge of the six methods is as an aid in thinking of a controlling idea. In Chapter 2, where we discussed the steps which you should follow in order to write a good paragraph, we placed consideration of development *after* choice of a controlling idea. You were told (1) to choose a topic, (2) to choose a controlling idea, (3) to express this idea in a good topic sentence, and *then* (4) to proceed with development of the controlling idea.

When you write, you may choose to continue to follow this pattern. However, now that you are familiar with six methods of developing your material in a paragraph, you may be able to put this knowledge to work earlier than we had indicated. Whenever you are finding it difficult to think of anything to say about a topic you want to write on—or *must* write on—let your mind run over the six methods you know in order—from example to process analysis. A consideration of each in connection with your topic may actually help you come up with a controlling idea for your paragraph.

For instance, suppose that one of the topics you are considering for a paragraph is "cybernetics." You select this topic because you know a little about it and find it interesting. However, you cannot decide precisely what to say about it, how to focus your paragraph. Consider the six methods. If you use example, the first method, could you get across a message about cybernetics? After careful analysis, you decide that you have enough knowledge of the subject to give several examples of the role which cybernetics plays in our lives today, and you consider using the following topic sentence:

Cybernetics plays a prominent role in our lives today.

But before you reach a final decision, you consider the next method, definition, and you realize that you could also develop a paragraph in which you define the term *cybernetics*. Because most people do not know what the word means, you decide that a paragraph developed by definition would be more meaningful to most readers than a paragraph developed by example. After considering the other four methods, you find that you cannot use any of them as well as you can definition, and you decide to develop a paragraph devoted to a formal definition of the term *cybernetics*. You then write a new topic sentence that reflects this decision:

Many people may have heard of the term *cybernetics,* but probably few know what it means.

Keep in mind, of course, that when you choose a controlling idea on the basis of a review of the six methods of paragraph development, the question of which method to use in developing your paragraph is also automatically answered. You will use the method that suggested the controlling idea to you.

Choosing the Best Method for Developing a Paragraph

There will be times when selecting a controlling idea for a paragraph is no problem at all. After reviewing a potential list of topics, you may realize that you have something worthwhile to say about one of them. You know *what* you are going to say; your problem is deciding *how* to say it. In this situation, a review of the six methods of development is in order. It will be your task to decide which method will work best for you.

Suppose, for example, that you plan to write on the topic "gun control," and you know that you want to say that gun control would benefit society. When you go over the options you have for paragraph development, you may find that any of the six methods could be used but that either comparison and contrast or cause and effect seems to be the most suitable. If you know whether gun control in another country has reduced crime there, you can compare the crime rate in that country to crime in the United States. On the other hand, you can choose to support your controlling idea by showing the effects of the relatively free circulation of guns in our country—that is, the effects, or results, of the *absence* of gun control. You decide, finally, that you can most effectively use the information and ideas you have about this controversial topic in a paragraph that deals with effects.

SUMMARY

1. If you are having trouble deciding on a controlling idea for a paragraph, a consideration of the six methods of development discussed in this chapter may help you select one.

2. After you have chosen a controlling idea, a consideration of the six methods should help you select the best method for developing your paragraph. Of course, if you have selected a controlling idea on the basis of a review of the methods of development, the method that suggested the controlling idea is the one that you would use.

EXERCISES

I. Examine each of the following topic sentences carefully. Review the six methods of development which you have studied in this chapter, and decide which would be the best for developing each topic sentence.

>   **A.** Why is the bald eagle, our country's symbol, becoming an endangered species?
>
>   **B.** Along with the need to succeed, there exists in almost everyone an opposite need to avoid success.
>
>   **C.** Music surrounds us every day of our lives.
>
>   **D.** Conservation is the wise use of natural resources.
>
>   **E.** American society degrades and neglects the elderly.
>
>   **F.** There are many effective ways to deal with sleeplessness without having to resort to drugs.
>
>   **G.** Habits are actions which a person performs regularly and unconsciously.
>
>   **H.** The student union houses many different groups of people.

II. Read each of the paragraphs below carefully. For each paragraph answer the following questions:

>   **1.** Which of the six methods of development do you think the writer was attempting to use?
>
>   **2.** Was the effort successful? If not, state what other method of development could have been used more effectively, and why.

>   **A.** Most men have, it would seem, one of two attitudes toward women. And these attitudes—chauvinism and nonsexism—are as reflective of the male psyche as a mirror is of a man's appearance. The chauvinist male believes that he is superior to women in intelligence, strength, and emotional stability. Raised in an environment which toughened him while it coddled women, he truly believes that females are inferior objects to be treated with gloved hands. The concept of equality is often so alien to the male chauvinist that he can never put down his guard long enough to give the opposite sex a chance to prove its worth. This type of sexist man, while appearing to be strong, is actually concealing fears of his own inadequacy. In contrast, the nonsexist male believes that women are equal to him in intelligence, strength, and emotional stability. However he was raised, the "new man"

is looking toward a future when members of the opposite sex will work and live alongside him as equals. The nonsexist male, although possibly considered naive by some people, is secure enough in his masculinity to respect and admire femininity. Instead of fearing inadequacy, he recognizes that we are all inadequate at times, just as all people—male and female—are strong at times.

B. A student can be either a good student, an average student, or an "F" student. A good student does well on tests. He or she studies a great deal and is willing to sacrifice leisure time for additional study time. The average student rarely sacrifices all of his time to study, but he does receive the grade which he deserves—usually a "C." An "F" student is one who repeatedly flunks tests. An "F" student never finds time to study because he rarely tries to make time for schoolwork. A student can be someone who studies with effort, someone who studies with a little sacrifice, or someone who doesn't care at all about grades. Thus, a student can be classified as either a good student, an average student, or an "F" student.

C. Heavy social drinkers and back-alley drunks have several characteristics in common. First of all, the heavy social drinker sees every cocktail party and Saturday-night social as an excuse for becoming inebriated. He is not looked down on by his peers since they are well aware of the pressures put on him during a hard week at work. Likewise, the back-alley drunk saves his money during the week so that he can spend it on his Saturday-night binge. With "booze" in hand, he finds his favorite spot to settle down in and proceeds to drink himself into a stupor. By becoming thoroughly intoxicated, he can forget everyday trials and tribulations, slipping instead into alcoholic fantasies of success and contentment. Second, the heavy social drinker takes his whiskey and water with companions of similar social status. He and his friends discuss business, community issues, and current world events. In the same manner, the back-alley drunk and his cohorts exchange hard-luck stories and tales of the "good old days" while becoming intoxicated on cheap liquor. Finally, the hangover which they experience the day after a drinking spree awakens both the social drinker and the back-alley drunk to reality. With a splitting headache, the social drinker is forced to meet the daily obligations which his family and job require while he awaits the next excuse to become drunk. The socially outcast drunk awakens to reality either on a city street or in a back alley. He, too, exists from day to day, awaiting the next time he can drink himself into unconsciousness. The settings may be different, but the intentions of the heavy social drinker and the back-alley drunk are the same. Both wish to escape the reality of life for a few forgetful hours of drunken existence.

D. Laughter is a way of releasing inner tensions, and there are many classes and types of laughs. A happy laugh can be heard when someone finally passes an important examination which he studied for all night. It can also be heard coming from a small child running with his dog through the meadows. An inexperienced driver may find himself laughing when he tries to turn the steering wheel but ends up turning on the signal lights. His laughter stems from nervousness. The act of laughing helps him to relax. Then there is the sad laugh. This is the kind of laugh one experiences when watching a soap opera and finding out that George is leaving Helen for Jane who is married to Bob, George's brother-in-law. Laughter is the greatest of all emotional outlets.

E. *Autocross* is a one-person, one-car race against time through a small but difficult obstacle course. So small is an autocross course that the average-size parking lot will suffice for most races. Throughout the course are scattered pylons and other obstacles. These create sharp turns that are extremely difficult to maneuver a car between, especially when the car is moving quickly. The cars used in autocross must be small and agile if they are to negotiate the course effectively, but they must also have a great deal of horsepower. To shift and steer between the pylons, an autocross driver must have split-second timing. While shifting and steering, the driver must watch the course carefully. Even a single distraction can cause a driver to lose track of the course.

F. When trying to save the life of a drowning person, one should follow a certain series of steps. After you have gotten the victim out of the water, place him on his stomach, and give three quick upward back thrusts. This action removes water from the lungs. Next, turn the victim on his side and clear his mouth of any foreign materials. This procedure guarantees that the airway to the lungs is open. Then take the victim's head in the palm of one hand and tilt the head backwards. This step opens an air passageway. Next, take the index finger and thumb of your free hand and pinch the victim's nostrils closed. Then place your mouth securely over the victim's mouth and breathe into the victim's lungs.

Finally, place the heel of one hand on the top of the other and compress the center of the victim's chest. Repeat this procedure five times. It massages the heart and circulates the oxygen which you have forced into the victim's lungs. Then look to see if the victim is breathing on his own. If you cannot detect any breathing, repeat the entire process. Even if the patient recovers, transport him to the nearest hospital for further medical attention.

G. Sometimes a very bright child will deliberately fail in school because he fears the way his peers respond to his intelligence. Jealous of his intelligence, the other students have teased him, or worse still, condemned him for his success. Left out of the activities of other children, the bright child comes to feel that good grades are directly responsible for the behavior of his peers toward him. As a result, the child pretends not to know the answers to questions he is asked in class. He intentionally allows his grades to fall so that his peers will cease being jealous of him and will begin to socialize with him again. Happy with his popularity, the child allows his grades to drop even lower. He may even lose interest in his studies altogether, failing subjects which he could easily excel in.

H. Millions of Americans sit before their televisions daily and are brainwashed every ten minutes by a blaring commercial. Stupid though they may seem, these commercials greatly influence the habits and desires of the American public. Pretty girls smile, displaying their shiny white teeth, and millions rush out to buy the smile, or to "put their money where their mouths are" with a mouthwash. Housewives use Tide because they are told it will make the laundry cleaner, and teenagers who are told that they belong to "the Pepsi generation" buy "un-colas." Young people dressed in bathing suits convince adults and teenagers alike that they should buy Dr. Pepper because "he's a Pepper," and "she's a Pepper," and you should "be a Pepper too!" Perhaps the biggest sell jobs are afternoon and Saturday commercials that interrupt cartoon time. Aimed at children from four to fourteen years of age, these ads hawk everything from dolls that wet, walk, and talk to trains that zoom around their tracks, planes that fly through the living room, and ships that dive in the bathtub. Dolls tell children to have Mom buy them new Barbie clothes; Yogi Bear sells tee shirts; and the label from the cereal that goes "snap, crackle, and pop" is a means to obtain marvelous prizes. Supposedly more educated than ever before, the American public continues to fall prey to the gimmicks and slogans which television commercials blast into their homes, and hardly a complaint is ever heard.

I. Anglers generally go about locating fish in one of three ways. Those who prefer to fish the same lakes day after day usually know from experience which are the choicest spots. Experience has taught them that bass lurk in the quietly flowing water behind a certain rock, that trout hide in the calm current near an undercut bank, or that crappie and bream inhabit the sanctuary of submerged roots below a dead tree. Because new fish are constantly moving into them, these places remain good even when they are heavily fished. Other fishermen use their eyes to locate fish. While wading through the water, sitting in a slowly moving boat, or remaining stationary on the shore, they scrutinize the water for signs of feeding fish, paying special attention to unusual ripples or waves which might indicate that their dinner lies beneath the surface in wait of a tempting worm or well-turned fly. Still other fishermen learn where the fish are because they study the structure of the lake or stream where they fish. They know that fish can usually be found off sandbars and shoals, and they know that deep holes and rocky shores are often the most productive places to fish, even in an otherwise unproductive lake.

III. Select one of the following topics. Construct a topic sentence, and then write a paragraph that supports it, using one of the six methods of development discussed in this chapter.

    A. bumper stickers

    B. popular customs (or folk customs)

    C. computers

    D. divorce

    E. signs

    F. bigots

    G. recreational vehicles

    H. summer school

    I. aging

IV. Write a paragraph on a topic of your own choosing. Use one of the methods of development discussed in this chapter.

Chapter 5

Achieving Coherence

Coherence means "sticking together." When a paragraph is coherent, the reader can move smoothly from sentence to sentence without becoming confused or losing the writer's train of thought. Coherence is achieved by arranging one's material in a logical order and by providing signals that help the reader understand the relationships between the ideas in the paragraph. If points are taken up in a disordered sequence, the reader will find it difficult to follow the writer's train of thought; if there are no guideposts along the way to indicate relationships between ideas, the reader may become totally lost. Achieving coherence is vital to effective communication.

In Chapters 3 and 4 we saw that the success of a paragraph depends to a great extent on how well the writer has followed the principles of paragraph unity and paragraph development. In a paragraph that is *unified,* all the supporting sentences back up the controlling idea, and the reader is not presented with any facts or ideas that do not belong in the paragraph. In a paragraph that is adequately *developed,* the writer has selected one of the methods of development as a means of examining his subject and has followed that method consistently throughout the paragraph.

However, a paragraph may be unified and well developed *but still not be coherent.* The appropriate parts may be there, but they may not fit together well enough for the paragraph's overall message to be fully understandable to the reader. Consider, for example, the following paragraph:

(1) The current population explosion could yield devastating problems in the future. (2) Famine is already a serious problem in many countries. (3) If present trends continue, famine will spread. (4) The world population is rapidly outgrowing its limited food supply. (5) Famine could someday engulf most of the planet. (6) Millions of people would die daily. (7) In such a situation, full-scale wars would erupt. (8) Countries would struggle to expand their borders. (9) They would also try to take over new areas. (10) Food crops would be closely guarded and rationed. (11) Inflation would be intense. (12) Even people in higher income brackets would not be able to buy sufficient food. (13) The hungry would grow angry. (14) The anger of the hungry would cause riots to break out. (15) Man's full military power would be unleashed. (16) Countries would be torn apart by internal strife and rioting. (17) Those countries would begin looking to neighboring lands for natural resources and food. (18) Civilization as we know it would perish with a big boom.

This paragraph is unified: all the sentences back up the controlling idea, or, more specifically, all the details the sentences contain lend direct or indirect support to the assertion that the population explosion *could yield devastating problems in the future.* And the paragraph is adequately developed: the writer has selected a method of development, cause and effect, and has followed it throughout.

But the paragraph is not coherent. Specifically, three essential elements of coherence are missing:

1. The paragraph lacks any sense of *order,* or *organization.* The writer has used ideas that together adequately support his controlling idea and has chosen to develop his topic by showing how a *cause*—overpopulation—may lead to several *effects* —famine, inflation, and war. But he has not arranged his supporting information according to a logical plan.

2. The paragraph lacks *transitions*—that is, signals that serve as a link between one sentence and the next. A paragraph is made up of a number of separate sentences, of course, but we usually do not think of each sentence as a distinct unit. Rather, as we read, we look for clues that help us cross sentence boundaries by showing how the ideas in one sentence relate to those in the next.

3. The paragraph lacks any *sentence combining.* As you probably noticed, it contains a number of short sentences. If the ideas in short sentences are closely related, they may be better understood when they are combined into one longer sentence that makes the relationship clear. This technique also makes a paragraph less choppy and therefore more pleasing to read.

With all these elements of coherence missing, the *reader* will have to rearrange the ideas and discover the appropriate relationships between them if he is to get at what the writer is saying. And the reader will probably be too annoyed by the paragraph to bother.

Following is a second version of the same paragraph, revised to correct the defects we have noted:

> (1) The current population explosion could yield devastating problems in the future. (2) The world's population is rapidly outgrowing its limited food supply, and famine is already a serious problem in many countries. (3) If present trends continue, famine will spread and could someday engulf most of the planet, resulting in the deaths of millions of people daily. (4) In such a situation, what food crops remained would be closely guarded and rationed. (5) In addition, inflation would be so intense that even people in higher income brackets would not be able to buy sufficient food. (6) The hungry, in time, would grow angry, and their anger would cause riots to break out. (7) Eventually, countries torn apart by internal strife and rioting would begin looking to neighboring lands for natural resources and food. (8) Full-scale wars would erupt as the strife-torn countries struggled to expand their borders and take over new areas. (9) And finally, with man's full military power unleashed, civilization as we know it would perish with a big boom.

In this paragraph, the writer has arranged the events he is predicting in the order in which they might be expected to occur—that is, according to *time order.* Such a plan of organization is logical and natural because we perceive our everyday experience, our past, and our future to be made up of a sequence of events in time.

In addition, the sentences are now connected by a number of linking devices: repetition of key words (such as *problem, food*); repetition of key ideas through synonyms or closely related words (such as *riots, strife, rioting*); transitional words and phrases (such as *and, in addition, eventually,* and *finally*); and pronouns (such as *their,* in sentence 6, which refers back to "the hungry"). These connective devices bind the sentences in the paragraph together, making them a more coherent whole.

In the revised paragraph, the writer has also joined together short, choppy sentences to form longer sentences. The result is not only that his writing is more pleasing to read but also that the relationships between his thoughts are clearer. For example, the three sentences on famine in the original paragraph (sentences 3, 5, and 6) have been united into one sentence in the revised paragraph (sentence 3). This new sentence not only eliminates the repetition and choppiness of the original three sentences but also clarifies the relationship the writer sees between existing famine and future catastrophe.

Writers who order or organize their material logically and naturally, who use transitional devices where necessary, and who combine closely related thoughts in clearly developed sentences, will usually construct coherent paragraphs. In this chapter we will examine these three essentials of good expository writing.

Order

As we pointed out in Chapters 1 and 2, an expository paragraph begins with a general statement—the topic sentence—and then continues with supporting sentences that provide specifics to back up the topic sentence. This is the overall outline, or plan, that you have been using to write your paragraphs. But you have not been asked to think about the order in which your supporting sentences are arranged. A paragraph is well organized if the ideas and events it considers are presented in the order which best shows the relationships between them. In the following three sections we will focus on three possible organizational patterns:

1. time order
2. space order
3. order of importance

In some instances, the specific order you choose for the support in your paragraphs will depend on your controlling idea and on the method of development you have selected to support your controlling idea. For instance, a process analysis paragraph will usually involve time order for its support. In most cases, however, the organizational patterns listed above can be employed with any method of development.

Time Order

Time order, also called *chronological order,* simply means that events considered in a paragraph are arranged in the order in which they occurred or in which the reader would expect them to occur. A four-year-old child chanting "October, February, June, January, July" violates an order his older listeners take for granted. We would call his list disorganized or confused because it does not follow the established sequence of the months of our calendar. Similarly, readers expect that a paragraph focusing on a series of events will take up the events in chronological order and feel that it is disordered if it does not seem to do so.

The following paragraph, which presents directions for preparing and eating burritos, is developed by process analysis with supporting steps arranged according to time order:

Burritos are as easy to make as they are fun to eat. First, take a package of frozen tortillas out of the freezer, remove the tortillas, and place them on a cookie sheet. Preheat the oven to 400°, place the tortillas in the oven, and bake them until they are moist. Then brown one pound of hamburger meat mixed with onion and chili seasoning. While the hamburger is browning, empty an eight-ounce can of pinto beans into a saucepan and heat them on the stove. While the beans are warming, grate four ounces of cheddar cheese, shred one quarter of a head of lettuce, and chop two tomatoes into small pieces. When all of the ingredients—the tortillas, the browned hamburger meat, the pinto beans, the cheese, the lettuce, and the tomatoes—are ready, it is time to put the burrito together. Lay each tortilla out flat. Now put some of the warm beans onto the tortilla, and spread a small amount of hamburger on top of the beans. Sprinkle the cheese over the hamburger, and top it with the lettuce and tomatoes. To enjoy a burrito, you must learn the trick of folding the tortilla so that the mixture inside will not fall out. First fold the bottom flap up, then the right side over, and finally the left side over. Now it's time to eat and enjoy!

Imagine the confusion if the writer had told the reader to insert the hamburger before it was browned or if the writer had left out a step —say, preheating the oven. In a successfully ordered process analysis paragraph, one step leads to the next, in succession, and the information provided in one step may enable us to understand how to carry out the next step.

Paragraphs developed by process analysis, like the one on burritos, almost always involve time order. But time order can also appear in paragraphs using any other method of development. The cause-and-effect paragraph on page 110 is organized by time order, as is the following paragraph, developed by the use of example:

Job applicants who are well qualified for the position they are seeking sometimes fail to be hired because of a slip they make before or during the interview. For example, some candidates do not dress properly. One applicant may appear for an interview in clothes that are much too casual to convey a sense of respect for the job to a prospective employer. Another may make a bad impression by overdressing for an interview. There are applicants who, although dressed tastefully, arrive five or ten minutes late for an interview, only to find that the interviewer has moved on to the next candidate. Then there are applicants who talk too much during an interview. In their eagerness to please, they are entirely too chatty and end up annoying the interviewer. And, finally, when the interview turns to the question of salary, there are the applicants who appear more interested in this aspect of the job than in the duties they will have to perform. Such applicants may impress the potential employer as being self-seeking rather than committed to hard work.

In providing examples of reasons that qualified job applicants are sometimes not hired, the writer *first* points to failure to dress properly, *then* to arriving late for the interview, *then* to being too talkative, and *finally* to showing too much interest in money. Because these mistakes are presented in the order in which they are likely to be made, the paragraph's organization seems logical and natural to the reader.

In the paragraph that follows, time order is used to organize a paragraph developed through cause and effect:

> Injuries may harm an athlete physically, but worse than the physical discomfort they create is the psychological damage they sometimes bring. Even for minor injuries the athlete must undergo such treatments as ice baths, whirlpool baths, and retaping, all of which require time and patience and often make the athlete feel annoyed with himself for not having avoided the injury. Nursing the injury along in a cast, on crutches, or in a sling, the athlete is forced to adapt to a totally different life style, one which he may find difficult to accept. Accustomed to warming up with the team and getting psyched up for the win, he must sit on the sidelines and be a spectator. He must watch and accept, and if, for instance, his team is losing a close game—one which he knows he could help them win—his anguish is even greater. If the athlete's injury is serious enough to require his sitting out an entire season, the depression he feels may cause the injured player to lose faith in himself and the people around him. As the season progresses and as the fans see the player hobbling around on crutches, he becomes just someone who was stupid enough to get himself hurt. Eventually, the player must even confront the changed attitudes of friends and acquaintances, whose respect and admiration often become indifference and annoyance. Sensing this change, the injured athlete, at first only resentful, may eventually become hostile, perhaps even avoiding his old athletic environment altogether.

In this paragraph, the writer concentrates on the effects of physical injury on an athlete's mental outlook. In ordering his support, he presents these effects in the sequence in which they are likely to occur, using this sequence to make his paragraph more coherent.

SUMMARY

1. You can make your paragraphs more coherent by ordering their support according to basic organizational patterns. Three common patterns are time order, space order, and order of importance.
2. Time order (or chronological order) means simply that the supporting elements in a paragraph—examples or causes, for instance

—are arranged in the order in which they occurred or in which the reader would expect them to occur.

3. In paragraphs ordered by time, you must be sure that your supporting points consistently follow a chronological sequence and that no important point is left out.

EXERCISES

I. The following topic sentence is followed by a series of supporting sentences. Arrange the supporting sentences according to the time sequence in which they are likely to occur.

> **Topic Sentence:** Learning to go up and down stairs on crutches takes time, but it is not as difficult as most people think.

1. The patient quickly brings the crutches up to the next step and braces himself.

2. While going down the stairs, the patient places the crutches on the first step beneath him.

3. He repeats this process of "leg first, then crutch" until reaching the top of the stairs.

4. The physical therapist slowly explains and demonstrates both procedures.

5. Going up the stairs, the patient steps on the first step with the unbroken leg.

6. The patient repeats this procedure of "crutch first, then leg" until reaching the bottom of the stairway.

7. The patient steps down with the unbroken leg, making sure to keep the broken leg slightly in front of the other in order to prevent stumbling on the stairs.

8. After the patient has experimented on the practice stairs, he realizes that it really isn't that difficult, even though there is a little time involved.

9. After the therapist demonstrates the processes, the patient must practice until sure they have been learned properly.

II. Using time order to organize your supporting sentences, write a paragraph on one of the following topic sentences. Be sure that your supporting points consistently follow a chronological sequence and that no important point is left out.

A. From start to finish, moving can be a grueling chore.

B. A solar (or lunar) eclipse is a sensational event to watch.

    C. Teaching someone to drive a car can tax the patience of even the best of friends.

    D. A handful of important inventions have changed the course of the world.

    E. Day in and day out, television is very much the same.

    F. Joining a fraternity or sorority involves the observance of certain rituals.

III. Using time order to organize your supporting sentences, write a paragraph on a topic of your own choice.

Space Order

The second way to organize the support in a paragraph is according to space order—that is, according to a spatial arrangement or pattern. If, for example, you are writing a paragraph about the benefits to handicapped students of the location of buildings on your campus, you might choose to order the paragraph according to the spatial arrangement of the campus. You might begin with a discussion of how the most important buildings are located in the center of the campus, where the most activity is, and then go on to a discussion of how outlying buildings are conveniently arranged around the center of campus so that handicapped students have easy access to them.

Like time order, space order can appear in paragraphs using any method of development. And because it enables your reader to *visualize* what you are describing, space order can be a particularly effective way to add coherence to your writing. In the following paragraph, developed by division, the supporting sentences are effectively arranged according to a spatial pattern:

> Each major section of Wisconsin is noted for the food it provides the nation. Bordered on the north by Lake Superior and on the east by Lake Michigan, the northeastern section of the state supports a thriving fishing industry. Every year thousands of tons of trout, salmon, perch, bass, and smelt from the region are harvested, processed, and eventually sold to the public. Indeed, few other areas in the country produce as much fish as northeastern Wisconsin. While the southeastern portion of Wisconsin also boasts a fishing industry, it is primarily noted for the fruit grown in its numerous orchards. Because it has milder winters and warmer summers than the northern part of the state, southeastern Wisconsin has a climate ideally suited to raising peaches, apples, cherries, and other fruits. The southwestern section of Wisconsin, on the other hand, is one of the most famous grain-producing areas in the world. Its rich soil, watered by frequent rains and warmed by long summers, is perfect for the growing of wheat, barley, and especially

corn, the region's most important product. More rocky than the south-western part of the state, the northwestern section of Wisconsin earns the state the title "America's Dairyland." Every day the thousands of cows that graze on the gently rolling hills and slopes of northwestern Wisconsin produce millions of gallons of milk, much of which is proc-essed into butter, cream, or cheese. Like the other regions of Wisconsin, this area has an identity all its own, created at least in part by the food it produces.

The writer of this paragraph could simply have listed the many foods produced in Wisconsin. Instead, she divided the state into four sec-tions and discussed each region in terms of the food produced there. As a result, readers are able to "follow" the writer as she "moves" clockwise from region to region; they learn, moreover, that the state's food production and its geography are closely linked. The paragraph is more coherent than it would have been if the writer had merely listed food products one after another, and division of the food products according to a spatial arrangement is responsible for this added coherence.

The two types of order we have discussed so far are not mutually exclusive. A paragraph can be ordered by *both* time and space. Consider, for example, the following paragraph, developed by cause and effect, about the devastation an atomic bomb dropped on Chi-cago would create:

> If a fifty-megaton atomic bomb were dropped on Chicago, it would have a devastating effect on an area extending for several hundred miles around the point of blast. Almost instantly, the city itself would be an inferno of death and destruction. People in the downtown area would be killed immediately, and the buildings there would topple and disintegrate. Suburbs twenty-five miles to the north, the west, and the south of Chicago would feel the devastating effects of the bomb within minutes. Fire would destroy most of the buildings and people in those areas. Survivors of the fire would gradually be contaminated and de-stroyed by radiation. Within a few hours, crops and animals as far north as Milwaukee, Wisconsin, and as far south as Springfield, Illinois, would be poisoned by the spread of radiation outward from the blast. By hiding in bomb shelters and basements, a few people might manage to survive, but both farmland and water would contain high levels of radiation, making them useless for many years. Eventually, fallout from the bomb blast would radiate into all parts of the country, and cities as distant as Seattle and Miami would feel its effects.

The writer of this paragraph analyzes the effects of the explosion of an atomic bomb, ordering those effects according to both their chronological sequence and their spatial arrangement. He begins with a discussion of the immediate effects the bomb would have on the city itself, then analyzes the destruction the bomb would gradually inflict on the surrounding suburbs, and goes on to say that the bomb would eventually affect virtually every area of the country. Thus time order and space order work together to make this paragraph coherent.

SUMMARY

1. In paragraphs ordered by space, the writer organizes the support in the paragraph according to a spatial arrangement or pattern. Space order enables a reader to visualize what is being described.
2. Space order and time order are not mutually exclusive. The supports in a paragraph can, if the topic warrants it, be ordered by both space and time.

EXERCISES

I. Write a paragraph using one of the following topic sentences. Order your support according to space order. Remember to try to describe your supporting details so that your readers can visualize their spatial relationships. You may combine space and time order if you feel the topic warrants it.

A. The state of Pennsylvania is known for its historic landmarks.
B. A trip around Lake Michigan is a delightful experience.
C. From bumper to bumper, a large car is a better buy than a small car.
D. Many American cities depend on the Mississippi River for their livelihood.
E. Vegetable gardens are usually more productive if they are arranged with care.
F. Most supermarkets have a familiar layout.
G. Students sit in different parts of the classroom for a variety of reasons.
H. Almost every kind of climate can be found somewhere in the United States.
I. An old house frequently has a number of hidden problems.
J. The exploration of a battlefield can be an educational experience.

II. Using space order to order your support, write a paragraph on a topic of your own choosing.

Order of Importance

Still another way you can organize the supporting material in your paragraphs is to arrange your ideas according to their order of importance—that is, according to how strongly you wish to emphasize each one. With this method, you present the least important idea first, then the next most important, and so on until you end the paragraph with the most important idea. This method of ordering supporting sentences according to their relative importance is probably used more often in student and professional writing than the other methods of ordering paragraphs previously discussed. The reason for this is that so many different types of writing require building evidence to support points of view and to be convincing.

In the following paragraph, for instance, the writer uses the cause-and-effect method of paragraph development to discuss why many students dislike unannounced in-class writing assignments, and she organizes the ideas in her paragraph from least important to most important:

> Most students dislike spur-of-the-moment in-class writing assignments. In the first place, they may not have with them the kind of paper or pen which they like to use, and they are almost certain to find themselves without a dictionary. Second, students often find that if the choice of topic is left to them, they are unable, on such short notice, to think of anything worthwhile to write about. If, on the other hand, they are given a number of topics to choose from, they may not be able to think of enough to say about any of them. A still greater source of discomfort for many students is the classroom environment itself. Nervous students may be whispering, coughing, asking the teacher questions, or otherwise distracting those who are trying to concentrate. The most difficult problem with unannounced in-class writing assignments, however, is the pressure involved. In part, the pressure is a matter of time: students know that they have only forty-five or fifty minutes in which to produce a finished paragraph or essay, and every glance at the clock causes a rise on the pressure gauge. Being compelled to produce a well-written paragraph or essay on demand creates so much pressure, in fact, that some students are unable to write anything and therefore turn in a blank sheet of paper. Other students, feeling the pressure almost as much, submit a few indecisive sentences. And most students would admit that whatever writing they turn in is bound to be the worst they have produced during the semester.

In this paragraph the writer discusses causes for student dislike of in-class writing assignments in this order: lack of writing materials, difficulty in choosing a topic, classroom distractions, and the pressure to perform. By moving from a valid but mild cause, to more important factors, and finally to the most important cause, pressure, the writer achieves a coherent and convincing paragraph.

The following paragraph, developed by means of contrast, demonstrates how effective the use of an order-of-importance arrangement can be to the achievement of a coherent paragraph:

> Many differences existed between the two earliest political parties in the United States, the Federalist Party and the Republican Party. For one thing, the Federalists favored a loose interpretation of the Constitution. Although the Constitution does not specifically mention a bank, for instance, the Federalists argued that the power to establish one is implied. The Republicans, on the other hand, believed in a strict interpretation of the Constitution; they felt that only in extreme circumstances would it be acceptable to assume the power required for establishing a bank. A second, and perhaps more significant, difference between the two parties involved their attitudes toward the structure of government itself. The Federalists believed in a strong central government geared to serving the interests of the few. Conversely, the Republicans supported the concept of a weak central government, with its powers distributed among the many. This difference resulted from what was perhaps the most fundamental dissimilarity between the parties. The "rich, wise, and well-born" were basically Federalists. They felt that the average citizen was incapable of governing intelligently. The Republicans, for their part, *were* the average citizens. Thus the difference in background and philosophy of the members of the two parties underlay their different attitudes toward specific activities of the government and toward the very nature of government.

According to the writer, the fact that members of the Federalist Party were well-born while the members of the Republican Party were largely "average citizens" was the most fundamental difference between the two parties because it *underlay* the other differences in attitude and philosophy. Because he judges this difference to be most important, the writer has made it the culmination toward which the rest of the paragraph moves. The paragraph is convincing because the reader comes away with the most important support for the controlling idea clearly in his mind. Had the writer presented the other points randomly rather than according to their relative importance, the paragraph would have lacked coherence.

When you decide to arrange the supporting evidence in a paragraph according to order of importance, you may find it helpful to follow a specific procedure. After you have selected the primary supports for your controlling idea, list them according to their importance to you, with the most important point first, the next most important point second, and so on. If you have no more than three primary supports, you might make your list mentally. If you have more than three supports, though, you should write your list down. When you begin to write your paragraph, *reverse* your list and take up the least important point first; then move on up through your list so that you conclude your paragraph with the most significant point.

In this way the writer of the paragraph on in-class papers might have jotted down the following informal list of supports, giving the most important first:

1. pressure
2. noisy classroom
3. difficulty in finding a suitable topic
4. lack of writing materials

The finished paragraph, of course, takes up these points in reverse.

SUMMARY

1. Ordering the supports in a paragraph according to their relative importance is another way to make your paragraphs coherent. Order of importance is probably used more often than any other principle in the arranging of supports within a paragraph.
2. When you decide to order the supports in a paragraph according to order of importance, you should make a list of primary supports with your most important supports first, then the next most important, and so on to the least important. When you write the paragraph, reverse the list and order your supports from the least to the most important. Fill in secondary supports as needed.

EXERCISES

I. The first sentence in each group below is a topic sentence. The rest of the sentences in the group are the primary supports for a paragraph that develops the topic sentence. Rearrange the supports according to what you believe to be their order of importance, placing the most important first, the second most important second, and so on. Then reverse the order of your supports according to the way they would appear in the finished paragraph.

   A. Topic Sentence: There are many reasons for our college to institute a fall semester break.

      1. Students would have the opportunity to take a break from the constant pressure of classes and exams.

      2. Students could catch up on work for classes that they are behind in.

      3. Students would have the opportunity to spend a few days at home visiting with family and friends.

B. Topic Sentence: There are several reasons why I want to be a nurse.

    1. There are many job opportunities in the nursing profession.

    2. A nurse's work is highly varied.

    3. I have always been fascinated by the human body and its ability to repair and maintain itself.

    4. I like to help people who are in need of care.

C. Topic Sentence: There are many reasons why a music-performance major might drop out of college.

    1. College can't provide the experience a musician needs to be able to play with a professional orchestra or band.

    2. A musician has more difficulty developing important contacts in the insular setting of the college campus.

    2. A musician is not judged by what or how many schools he has attended.

II. Develop a set of primary supports for one of the following topic sentences; then rank each primary support according to its importance, beginning with the most important support and working down to the support of least importance. Then reverse the order of your supports according to the way they would appear in the finished paragraph.

A. Jogging is a worthwhile form of exercise.

B. An "A" on a paper means a great deal.

C. When choosing a college, one has to consider many points.

D. Student governments do a good deal (or do nothing) to improve life on campus.

E. Living at home while attending college has definite advantages.

F. I object to my roommate's habits.

Transitional Devices

As we pointed out in the introduction to this chapter, coherence can be achieved in three basic ways: through attention to order, through the use of transitional devices, and through effective sentence combining. In the first section we explained how order is achieved by arranging your material according to basic patterns of thought and experience which help to tie the parts of your paragraph together. Now we'll turn to the second factor in achieving coherence: transitional devices. There are many devices at your disposal for producing smooth and effective transitions from point to point in your writing. In this section, we will consider some of the more common ones:

1. transitional words and phrases
2. pronouns
3. repetition of key words and phrases

Transitional Words and Phrases

Transitional words and phrases—such as *but, therefore, in addition, for example,* and *on the other hand*—add coherence to your paragraphs by linking the ideas in one sentence with those in the next. Transitional expressions (as they are also called) act as reminders of what you have already said and as signals indicating where you are going. When used effectively, they can make the difference between an easy-to-understand paragraph and one which is difficult to follow. Without transitional words and phrases, writing tends to be choppy and awkward.

The following paragraph, for instance, does not use transitional words and phrases to bring out the relationship between the ideas the paragraph contains:

> (1) The owner or driver of an automobile in this state should know the traffic laws concerning accidents. (2) Anyone involved in an accident must remain at the scene until the police arrive. (3) He should give his name, address, and registration information to the other driver. (4) If the police are not present, someone should phone them as soon as possible. (5) If an officer is present, the drivers can supply the necessary information at the scene of the accident. (6) Accidents result in a great deal of damage and/or personal injury. (7) If there is damage to one of the cars in excess of $250 but no injury, the driver of that car must file a written report with the Department of Motor Vehicles within thirty days. (8) If there is also personal injury, both drivers have to file a report within five days. (9) People forget to file reports in the required time, and the result may be a severe fine. (10) It is important to know state laws concerning the responsibilities of the driver involved in an accident.

The sentences in this paragraph are arranged in a logical order, but the paragraph lacks signals which would help the reader see the relationship between the ideas.

Following is the same paragraph rewritten to include transitional words and phrases (shown in italics):

> (1) The owner or driver of an automobile in this state should know the traffic laws concerning accidents. (2) *For example,* anyone involved in an accident must remain at the scene until the police arrive. (3) *In addition,* he should give his name, address, and registration informa-

tion to the other driver. (4) If the police are not present, someone should phone them as soon as possible. (5) *But* if an officer is present, the drivers can supply the necessary information at the scene of the accident. (6) *Frequently,* accidents result in a great deal of damage and/or personal injury. (7) If there is damage to one of the cars in excess of $250 but no injury, the driver of that car must file a written report with the Department of Motor Vehicles within thirty days. (8) If there is also personal injury, both drivers have to file a report within five days. (9) *Often* people forget to file reports in the required time, and the result may be a severe fine. (10) *Therefore,* it is important to know state laws concerning the responsibilities of the driver involved in an accident.

Unlike the first version, this paragraph is easy to follow because transitional words and phrases provide the reader with signals to relate the sentences to each other.

Transitional words and phrases take many forms—so many, in fact, that a complete list of all or most of them would be unmanageably long. For your convenience, however, we have drawn up a list of those most frequently used, categorized according to their most common uses:

A. *Example*

occasionally, usually, often, frequently, especially, specifically, principally, mainly, namely, significantly, indeed, for example, for instance, first of all, for one thing, most important, to illustrate, in particular, in general

B. *Addition*

and, also, furthermore, first, second, third, next, other, besides, too, likewise, moreover, last, again, finally, in addition, in the first (second, third) place, what is more, as well, at last, next to

C. *Comparison*

similarly, likewise, like, as, at the same time, in the same way, in like manner

D. *Contrast*

but, however, yet, or, nevertheless, still, nonetheless, conversely, nor, rather, whereas, though, on the one hand, on the other hand, on the contrary, by contrast, in contrast, even though, at the same time

E. *Concession*

doubtless, surely, certainly, naturally, granted that, although this may be true, no doubt, I concede, I admit

F. *Repetition*

again, as has been pointed out, to repeat, in other words, as I have said above, once again

G. *Result*

then, therefore, thus, hence, so, consequently, as a result, all in all

H. *Conclusion*

finally, then, thus, hence, therefore, so, in conclusion, to sum up, to summarize, to conclude, in short

I. *Time*

before, earlier, formerly, afterward, later, subsequently, presently, soon, shortly, meanwhile, simultaneously, now, then, after a while, at last, at that time, in the meantime, in the past, until now

J. *Place*

here, there, elsewhere, above, below, behind, beyond, nearby, adjacent to, farther on, in the background, opposite to, to the right

Consult this list if you are having trouble thinking of transitional words and phrases, but use it with caution. Too many transitional words and phrases, or inappropriate ones, can be just as harmful as too few. *Be sure to select the word or phrase that links your ideas logically.* And *always remember to use only as many transitional words and phrases as are needed to make your paragraph coherent.*

SUMMARY

1. Transitional devices add coherence to a paragraph by linking the ideas in one sentence with those in the next. They remind the reader what preceded and signal what is to follow.
2. When used effectively, transitional words and phrases can make the difference between a clearly written and easy-to-read paragraph and one which is difficult to follow because it moves abruptly from sentence to sentence.
3. When selecting transitional words and phrases for your paragraphs, be sure to select only those that fit logically and to use only as many as are needed to make your paragraph coherent.

EXERCISES

I. Examine the following paragraphs and the lists below each. Choose the transitional word or phrase from each list which best fits into the indicated space.

    A. The primary cause of heart attack among men in their forties and fifties is a build-up of cholesterol in the bloodstream. Particularly among men who are overweight, don't exercise, and have high blood pressure, cholesterol tends to accumulate on the walls of the arteries that supply the heart muscle with oxygen and essential nutrients. The arteries may eventually become so congested with fatty deposits that blood flow is decreased or completely shut off. A significant decrease in the amount of blood flowing to the heart can cause severe arterial damage. (1)_____the worst damage occurs when the blood flow is completely stopped. When this happens, the area of the heart to which the blood was being pumped is cut off from its supply of oxygen and nutrients. (2)_____, the heart muscle in the receiving area cannot function, and a heart attack ensues. (3)_____, to prevent a heart attack, one should exercise and stay trim, but most of all one should avoid excessive intake of cholesterol.

      1. a. But   **2. a.** Occasionally
         b. Besides   **b.** Nonetheless
         c. As I have said above   **c.** Consequently
                3. a. For instance
                   b. Therefore
                 c. And

    B. The United States government should stop interfering with genetic research. (1)_____the government has to keep an eye on the type of experimentation being done, too rigid restrictions on genetic researchers discourage many efforts that could lead to a cure for certain diseases. (2)_____, scientists are trying to persuade the government to lift restrictions that prohibit them from working toward the discovery of the gene responsible for insulin production. If they could learn to synthesize this particular gene, they could eliminate the diabetic's need for a daily injection. (3)_____, some scientists believe that cancer and other diseases that are often fatal could be brought under control by genetic implantation. (4)_____, the government says no.

      1. a. Although   **2. a.** Secondly
         b. Next   **b.** Although

     c. Specifically   **c.** For instance

3. a. In addition   **4. a.** Consequently

     b. For instance   **b.** Nevertheless

     c. Although   **c.** As a result

II. From the list of transitional words and phrases (pp. 120–121), select the word or phrase that best fits in the indicated spaces. In each case, the *use* of the transitional expression is specified.

A. Our state's correctional system is plagued with problems. _____, high officials increase their personal wealth
(EXAMPLE)
by awarding building and catering contracts to disreputable companies in return for bribes._____, promo-
(ADDITION)
tions within the system are made on the basis of politics, not merit._____, the system is filled with people at the
(RESULT)
top who know little about what they are doing. _____, lackadaisical security measures, allowing
(ADDITION)
trusted inmates to control certain operations of the institution, are part of the growing plight. But one increasing tendency in particular is doing harm to the system's image and efficiency. That is the tendency of officials who are charged with important tasks and who make faulty decisions to cover up their mistakes._____, one would think that
(CONCLUSION)
amid all the strife some effort would be made to rectify these problems, but a seemingly dogged determination to resist change overshadows the system.

B. Of all the possessions successful bass fisherman must have, four are highly important: a solid rod, a reliable reel, the proper bait, and a large quantity of patience._____ _____, the rod should be approximately five and
(EXAMPLE)
one-half feet in length and should have the proper degree of rigidity. The eyelets should be lined up and smoothly sanded to ensure the proper flow of the line when it is cast. The reel,_____, must provide a smooth cast;
(COMPARISON)
otherwise its "drag" system will not function efficiently. _____, successful bass fishermen need the right
(ADDITION)
bait. While some fishermen prefer plastic worms and others "top water" and shallow diving lures, successful fishermen

know that the right kind of bait catches the most fish. _____, they must have vast amounts of patience. (ADDITION)

Bass fishermen may cast their baits for hours on end without so much as a strike. Fishermen who have patience, though, and refuse to give up may be rewarded with a fine day's catch.

III. From the list of transitional words and phrases (pp. 120–121), select the word or phrase which best fits each blank in the following paragraphs. Do not use the same transition more than once in any paragraph.

  A. A customer at a burger restaurant has to make a choice. "With or without?" the pleasant face behind the counter will ask. Before answering, one has to determine if he has enough time to put on his own condiments. If, _____, he is in a hurry, then most likely he will reply, "With." His reply will result in his quickly receiving a prepacked hamburger with dry lettuce, a soggy tomato slice, and warmed-over meat. He really doesn't care because he has to get back to work. So he pays for his meal, jumps into his car, and gulps the burger down on his way. If, _____, the burger buyer has plenty of time, then he will reply, "Without." This reply will result in his receiving a fresh burger off the grill to lavish with the kind and quantity of condiments he likes. If you wish to enjoy your meal, _____, avoid being in a hurry when you go to a burger restaurant.

  B. The regular meeting of the Parents' and Teachers' Association was held Thursday night at 7:30 P.M. in the school auditorium. _____, the parliamentarian called the meeting to order. The president _____ made her opening remarks and welcomed any guests. _____, the secretary called the officer's roll and took a count of members present. _____ the secretary read the minutes of the previous meeting. After the minutes were read, the president asked if there were any additions or corrections, and because there were none, the minutes stood approved as read. The minutes read and approved, the next item on the agenda was the treasurer's report. A financial statement was presented by the treasurer, and following the approval of the statement a vote was taken on whether the current bills on hand were to be paid. A unanimous vote of "yes" was recorded. _____ the meeting focused on new business, which included such items as upcoming elections, fund-raising activities, and other important issues. _____, after discussion had ended, the president asked for a motion that the meeting be adjourned.

C. Once you have set foot on Ireland's soil, you will never want to leave it. A land of many outstanding characteristics, Ireland has as its most striking quality a beautiful countryside. It contains, _____, a magnificent, flat-topped mountain, called Ben Bella, that hovers over the landscape. _____ the mountain there are rock-ribbed hills where for centuries flocks of sheep have grazed. _____ _____ lining these hills are rock fences, originally constructed as boundaries by farmers who cleared the rocks from their crop lands. _____, the traveler who wants natural beauty cannot visit a lovelier country than Ireland.

D. One of the most useful techniques in the sport of body building is called "supersetting." To understand supersetting, one must _____ understand that in weightlifting a "set" is the completion of a specified number of repetitions of an exercise. Supersetting, _____, is the practice of combining sets of exercises for muscles located on opposite sides of the body. _____, one would do a set of an exercise for the muscle on the front of the arm, the bicep, and ____ _____ proceed immediately to a set of exercises for the muscle located on the back of the arm, the tricep. Supersetting is valuable because it saves time. One can work two body parts in the time it would normally take to work one. _____, supersetting promotes cardiovascular fitness by placing a greater demand on the heart and lungs. A _____ advantage of supersetting is the sense of both stimulation and relaxation experienced when a part of the body is fully exercised.

Pronouns

Another device that acts as a link between sentences in a paragraph is the pronoun, a word used in place of a noun. The following pronouns are frequently used to add coherence to expository paragraphs:

	Singular	*Plural*
First Person	I	we
	me	us
	my, mine	our, ours
	myself	ourselves
Second Person	you	you
	your, yours	your, yours
	yourself	yourselves

Third Person	he, she, it	they
	him, her, it	them
	his, her, hers, its	their, theirs
	himself, herself, itself	themselves
Demonstratives	this, that	these, those

Pronouns add coherence to a paragraph in two ways: (1) they provide for smoother reading by eliminating the awkward and distracting repetition of nouns, and (2) they serve as links between parts of a paragraph by referring to a noun in a preceding or following sentence or sentence part.

The following paragraph focuses on the career of Hubert H. Humphrey. Naturally, the writer often refers to Humphrey by name, but imagine how awkward the paragraph would be if the writer repeated *Hubert H. Humphrey* (or even just *Humphrey*) time and again instead of substituting pronouns at the appropriate places. With the exception of *those* in sentence 3, all the pronouns in the paragraph refer to Humphrey:

> (1) Only after *his* death have some people come to realize the dedication of Hubert H. Humphrey. (2) Born in South Dakota, Humphrey claimed Minnesota as *his* home for most of *his* life. (3) *He* held many jobs, including *those* of pharmacist and teacher, but the real business of Humphrey's life began in 1944, when *he* became President Franklin Roosevelt's Minnesota campaign manager. (4) Thereafter, Hubert H. Humphrey was first, last, and always a politician. (5) After being elected mayor of Minneapolis in 1945, *he* plunged into national politics three years later when *he* shocked the Democratic National Convention and the nation with an impassioned plea for minority rights. (6) It appeared certain that Harry S Truman and the Democrats were headed for defeat in the 1948 election. (7) Truman, however, won the White House, and Hubert H. Humphrey captured the seat in the Senate that *he* was to hold for twenty-three years, with one interruption to be vice president. (8) Humphrey never won the presidency, though *he* tried several times and came close in 1968. (9) A devoted public servant, Hubert H. Humphrey considered *his* greatest achievement to be the enactment of the Civil Rights Act of 1964.

The writer's use of pronouns not only makes the paragraph as a whole read smoothly but also provides links between one sentence and another. Thus, the reader has no difficulty following the progression of ideas throughout the paragraph.

Take care not to overuse pronouns, however. Like transitional words and phrases, pronouns should be used only when they are needed to make your writing smoother. Notice, for example, that in the paragraph on Humphrey the writer has not replaced every instance of the name Hubert H. Humphrey with a pronoun. If overused, pronouns can be as awkward as the constant repetition of the nouns they replace.

A Word of Caution: Pronouns and Their Antecedents. The noun (or nouns) that a pronoun substitutes for (or, as we also say, *refers to*) is called the *antecedent* of the pronoun. When you use a pronoun in your writing, be sure that your reader will be able to identify its antecedent immediately. If your reader has to stop and hunt for a pronoun's antecedent, he or she may lose your train of thought. There are three types of pronoun-antecedent errors that writers are likely to make: *ambiguous reference, broad reference,* and *weak reference.*

An *ambiguous reference* occurs when there are two or more possible antecedents for a pronoun:

Unclear: Humphrey became President Roosevelt's Minnesota campaign manager in 1944. Without doubt, *he* was delighted with the job *he* did. [The antecedent for the pronoun *he* is ambiguous. *He* could refer to Humphrey or President Roosevelt or both.]

Clear: Humphrey became President Roosevelt's Minnesota campaign manager in 1944. Without doubt, *the president* was delighted with the job *Humphrey* did.

A *broad reference* occurs when a pronoun refers to an entire statement rather than to a specific noun or nouns:

Unclear: Humphrey's speech was poorly received by anti–civil rights forces. *This* was an indication of their hostile attitude. [The pronoun *this* is intended to substitute for the entire sentence preceding it. As a result, its antecedent is unclear.]

Clear: Humphrey's speech was poorly received by anti–civil rights forces. *The poor response* was an indication of their hostile attitude.

A *weak reference* occurs when the antecedent is a noun that cannot *logically* be replaced by the pronoun:

Unclear: Humphrey was at one time a teacher. *This,* of course, was not a job that was suited to his ambitions. [The pronoun *this* is intended to substitute for the word *teacher.* However, the reference is unclear because a "teacher" is not a "job."]

Clear: Humphrey was at one time a teacher. *Teaching,* of course, was not a job that was suited to his ambitions.

Finally, be sure when you use a pronoun that it agrees, or corresponds in form, with its antecedent in *person* (first, second, third), *number* (singular, plural), and, if possible, *gender* (masculine, feminine, neuter).

SUMMARY

1. Pronouns add coherence to a paragraph in two ways: they smooth the flow of sentences by eliminating awkward repetition of nouns, and they help to knit a paragraph together by referring to nouns in previous or following sentences or sentence parts.
2. Use pronouns only when they are needed to add coherence to your paragraph.
3. Be sure that every pronoun has a clear antecedent.
4. Be certain that every pronoun agrees with its antecedent in person, number, and, if possible, gender.

EXERCISES

I. In the following paragraphs, fill in the blanks with the appropriate pronouns. If necessary, refer to the list of pronouns (pp. 125–126).

    A. Human beings are destroying their environment. It is ironic how people pollute _____ surroundings and then go to great pains to clean up the messes that _____ have made. A cheap method of getting rid of industrial wastes is to dump _____ into rivers or lakes. The result of such intrusions into nature is the death of many forms of life in and around the waters. Only when the pollution reaches _____ reservoirs, however, do people figure that the time has come to clean up _____ environment. Then _____ create a series of expensive projects to restore the water to _____ original purity. Of course, the cheapest and most effective way to get clean water is not to pollute _____ in the first place.

    B. A mother robin's lot is not a happy one. Having found a baby female robin that was not yet out of _____ pin feathers, _____ family and I decided to try to fulfill the role of motherhood. _____ carried _____ into the house, being careful not to break a wing, and made a nest for _____ out of old rags laid in an Easter basket. _____ named _____ "Bottomless." _____ seemed the only fitting name, considering the number of worms _____ could consume in a single day. Gathering worms for _____ fosterchild and then feeding _____ to _____ were among the most difficult tasks confronting _____. _____ also found later on that teaching _____ to find _____ own worms and then leaving "Bottomless" on _____ own to learn how to fly was equally difficult. Most difficult for _____, however, was coping with _____ feelings when one day, after _____ had learned to fly, "Bottomless" did not come home.

C. People who smoke in nonsmoking areas are _____ who irritate me the most. _____ have absolutely no respect for _____ and other people who are sitting around _____. In restaurants, for example, _____ often invade nonsmoking sections where nonsmokers have sought refuge from the smoke. Once in the nonsmoking area, these people light up and, when not sneaking a puff, clandestinely hold _____ cigarettes under the table. The result is, of course, that the smoke still circulates, and anyone who cannot stand _____ must either wear a gas mask or leave before _____ food is served.

II. The following exercise demonstrates the importance of furnishing clear antecedents for each pronoun you use. Read the paragraphs below carefully, and determine what word each underlined pronoun refers to. If there is a problem of pronoun reference, decide whether the pronoun has an *ambiguous, broad,* or *weak* reference.

A. (1) I enjoy working with handicapped children because they look up to me as a parent figure. (2) The children are always asking me to watch what they are doing, and they inevitably quiz me on how well I thought they did. (3) Usually I show a great deal of enthusiasm and offer constructive aid. (4) *This,* of course, results in a great deal of respect from the children. (5) It seems that non-handicapped children never appreciate my efforts as much as the handicapped children do. (6) And when I am successful in helping a handicapped child complete a task or confront a problem, I feel a great deal of satisfaction. (7) *This* is why working with the handicapped is so rewarding to me.

B. (1) Physical punishment and verbal abuse in the classroom frequently have adverse effects on children. (2) Despite the common belief that a few smacks on the behind never hurt anyone, children who are slapped or beaten by teachers may be left with both physical and mental scars. (3) Often *they* are so mad at *them* that *they* are unaware of *their* own strength. (4) Many times *this* results in serious injuries and permanent handicaps. (5) Tongue-lashings, too, can wound a sensitive child. (6) If a teacher scolds a child by calling *him* dumb or slow, *that* is unfortunate. (7) Children often believe what their teachers say and grow up thinking that *they* are stupid. (8) Often it takes years to reverse the thinking, and *that* sets the child back even further.

Repetition of Key Words and Phrases

Repetition of key words and phrases is another transitional device you can use to achieve coherence in your paragraphs. We do not mean to suggest, of course, that words and phrases should be repeated so often that they begin to annoy the reader. We are saying, rather, that to maintain focus on your controlling idea, you can repeat particular words and phrases that emphasize this idea. The paragraph below, for instance, keeps the focus on its controlling idea—the importance of the multivitamin in a child's diet —by either repeating certain key words or using closely related phrases:

> The *multivitamin* plays an important role in a child's diet. Laboratory tests show that most children do not obtain the recommended daily allowances of *vitamins* and minerals from the food they eat. To maintain and build healthy bodies, therefore, most children need a *dietary supplement.* One *multivitamin* each day provides the *vitamins* A, B-6, B-12, C, D, and E, as well as folic acid, thiamine, riboflavin, niacin, and even iron. For children who do not eat a well-balanced diet or who are unable to absorb essential *vitamins* and minerals from their regular meals, a single *supplementary tablet* may ensure good health.

In this paragraph, repetition of the words *multivitamin* and *vitamins* keeps the focus of the paragraph clear. To avoid too much repetition, though, the writer also uses two closely related phrases: *dietary supplement* and *supplementary tablet.* These phrases add variety to the paragraph. They also add coherence because they echo the key words around which the paragraph is structured.

Again, we do not wish to tell you to repeat words and phrases needlessly. Rather, our intention is to remind you to look back over your paragraphs to make sure that, where appropriate, you have used repetition of a key word, or have introduced a closely related phrase or a synonym for a key word, to help focus the reader's attention on your controlling idea.

SUMMARY

1. To maintain focus on the controlling idea throughout a paragraph, writers often repeat key words and phrases that emphasize this idea.

2. Repetition of key words and phrases—either the original words, related forms, or synonyms—adds coherence to a paragraph by drawing the reader's attention to the controlling idea of the paragraph.

EXERCISES

I. Underline all key words and phrases that are repeated in the following paragraphs. Also underline variations of key terms.

   A. The escalating price of oil imported from other countries has had some beneficial effects on the United States. In the first place, our technology has been forced to develop faster than it might otherwise have developed. A good example of such technological progress is the advancements we have made in the fields of solar and nuclear energy. A second benefit of the hike in oil prices has been the increased number of jobs available to American workers. Exploration for new oil fields accounts for many of the new jobs. Offshore drilling, too, has resulted in a boost in the job market. Most important, though, the escalating price of imported oil has made the people of the United States realize that we must become independent of oil-supplying nations that might take advantage of our need.

   B. *Lamaze,* a word that sounds exotic, actually refers to something quite practical: a method of prepared childbirth. Lamaze classes teach the expectant mother and father methods of coping with the birth process. The mother, first of all, learns breathing and hand-motion techniques to aid her during labor. These techniques often enable the mother to undergo "natural childbirth," or childbirth without anesthesia. In addition, Lamaze classes instruct her in how to deal with such problems as "back labor" or even an emergency delivery. The husband is also trained: he is shown how to oversee his wife's breathing techniques, to time her contractions, and generally to offer moral support to her efforts. Lamaze classes, which are intended for women in their last months of pregnancy (and for their husbands), are usually taught by registered nurses with Lamaze certification.

   C. One of the major causes of our city's traffic problems is Main Street. To begin with, the street is not wide enough to handle the flow of traffic which plagues midtown. The midtown area has expanded vastly in the last few years, and the number of vehicles traveling through it has grown. Furthermore, there is an inadequate number of traffic lights on Main Street. For example, the very busy intersection at Second Avenue, where traffic flowing onto Main Street is always backed up, is greatly in need of a traffic light. There is also an urgent need to improve the condition of the street itself. There are numerous potholes that slow vehicles down, impeding the flow of traffic even further.

D. Television furnishes an effective means of advertising. One of the reasons for its effectiveness is simply that millions of Americans view television every day. It is estimated that the average American family watches television four hours a day. Second, television is more effective than, say, radio because television can appeal to the prospective buyer through both ear and eye. Viewers who can see the product that is being sold are more likely to buy it. And, finally, television advertising in the last ten years has become so sophisticated that television advertisers have been able to determine what kinds of audiences watch at specific times of the day. They can now air commercials that appeal specifically to the audience watching at any given time, and the result is, of course, that their pitches are more successful than when they promote their products randomly.

E. Getting a dog creates several duties for the owner. First of all, feeding the new pet regularly is necessary to his well-being. A puppy needs to be fed twice a day, as opposed to an adult dog, who needs feeding only once a day. Second, a healthy dog requires regular exercise. Taking him for daily walks or allowing him to run for lengthy periods of time increases his chances for good health and a sound muscular structure. Exercise also helps the dog to release the tension that builds up while he is confined. Finally, the dog must be protected from disease and health problems and therefore requires occasional trips to the veterinarian's office. He should be inoculated against distemper and rabies, as well as tested for worms and skin ailments.

Combining Sentences

The first two sections of this chapter have focused on two important means of achieving coherence in your paragraphs: arranging your supporting sentences in a logical and consistent order and furnishing transitional devices where needed. Still another way to achieve coherence is to combine two or more short, single-idea sentences into a longer sentence which will relate the ideas clearly and more effectively. Particularly if your sentences tend to be choppy, this method can help.

Consider, to begin with, the following paragraph, which consists of brief, simple sentences:

(1)The kangaroo rat is an interesting case study in survival. (2)It is found in North American deserts. (3)It is a member of the rodent family. (4)It is barely two inches high. (5)The kangaroo rat has enormous feet. (6)These enormous feet enable it to run on shifting sand. (7)It also has a tufted tail. (8)The tufted tail furnishes protection against blowing sand. (9)That tail is three times as long as the rat itself. (10)The kangaroo rat eats only seeds and grasses. (11)Seeds and grasses are abundant in the areas the kangaroo rat inhabits. (12)The rat itself is one of the main foods of all desert carnivores. (13)Some desert carnivores are snakes, owls, coyotes, and badgers. (14)The kangaroo rat is in many respects like all other desert animals. (15)It has adapted to desert life. (16)It has speed. (17)It has craftiness. (18)These traits, at times, enable it to outwit its pursuers.

This paragraph lacks the coherence readers expect in a well-written paragraph. It contains a clear controlling idea (an interesting case study in survival), possesses a specific method of development (example), and follows a logical order (order of importance). But because all the sentences in the paragraph are short and choppy, the reader encounters so many stops and starts that the sentence-to-sentence continuity of thought may be lost. For instance, the relationship between the ideas contained in sentences 14 and 15 is not clear. The reader does not know whether the author intends to develop the notion that the kangaroo rat "is like all other desert animals" or plans to open up a new line of thought in sentence 15.

To remedy the problem that the paragraph on the kangaroo rat poses, the writer reconstructed the sentences so that the relationships among thoughts became clear. He combined short sentences into longer ones which emphasized what needed to be emphasized and subordinated what needed to be subordinated. The following chart demonstrates how he unified his sentences for greater coherence and clarity.

Simple sentence	*changed to*	*in final sentence*
1. The kangaroo rat is an interesting case study in survival.	(main clause)	The kangaroo rat, a member of the rodent family found in North American deserts, is an interesting case study in survival.
2. It is found in North American deserts.	(phrase)	
3. It is a member of the rodent family.	(phrase)	

Simple sentence	changed to	in final sentence
4. It is barely two inches high.	(dependent clause)	Even though it is barely two inches high, the kangaroo rat has enormous feet for running on shifting sand and a tufted tail, which is three times as long as the rat itself, for protection against blowing sand.
5. The kangaroo rat has enormous feet.	(main clause)	
6. These enormous feet enable it to run on shifting sand.	(phrase)	
7. It also has a tufted tail.	(main clause)	
8. The tufted tail furnishes protection against blowing sand.	(phrase)	
9. That tail is three times as long as the rat itself.	(dependent clause)	
10. The kangaroo rat eats only seeds and grasses.	(phrase)	In spite of the fact that the kangaroo rat eats only the seeds and grasses abundant in the areas it inhabits, the rat itself is one of the main foods of desert carnivores, such as snakes, owls, coyotes, and badgers.
11. Seeds and grasses are abundant in the areas the kangaroo rat inhabits.	(phrase)	
12. The rat itself is one of the main foods of all desert carnivores.	(main clause)	
13. Some desert carnivores are snakes, owls, coyotes, and badgers.	(phrase)	
14. The kangaroo rat is like all the other desert animals.	(phrase)	Like all the other desert animals, it has adapted to desert life; its speed and craftiness, at times, enable it to outwit its pursuers.
15. It has adapted to desert life.	(main clause 1)	
16. It has speed.	(main clause 2)	
17. It has craftiness.	(main clause 2)	
18. These traits, at times, enable it to outwit its pursuers.	(main clause 2)	

When the final sentences are combined, the following paragraph is the product:

(1)The kangaroo rat, a member of the rodent family found in North American deserts, is an interesting case study in survival. (2)Even though it is barely two inches high, the kangaroo rat has enormous feet for running on shifting sand and a tufted tail, which is three times as long as the rat itself, for protection against blowing sand. (3)In spite of the fact that the kangaroo rat eats only the seeds and grasses abundant in the areas it inhabits, the rat itself is one of the main foods of desert carnivores, such as snakes, owls, coyotes, and badgers. (4)Like all the other desert animals, it has adapted to desert life; its speed and craftiness, at times, enable it to outwit its pursuers.

Obviously, this paragraph is clearer than its original version. In addition, the way in which these statements are linked emphasizes the relative importance of the ideas in each as they relate to the controlling idea of the paragraph. The fact that the kangaroo rat has enormous feet and a tufted tail receives the main emphasis in sentence 2 because these are the features of the rat which the writer wishes to point out as interesting and instrumental in survival. Thus, these facts are presented in the main clause of the sentence. The other information in the sentence—the fact that the kangaroo rat is barely two inches high and that the tail of the rat is three times as long as the rat—is linked to the main ideas in the sentence by means of dependent clauses; this information is important, but only as it relates to the more important information contained in the main clause of the sentence.

The point of all of this discussion is, of course, that the original sentences, when combined, not only retain their original meaning but take their appropriate places in the presentation of ideas in the paragraph—they are emphasized or subordinated through the way in which they are combined. As a result of similar combinations of the other sentences in the original paragraph, the final sentences in the revised paragraph are less monotonous, and the ideas are more clearly presented.

A Word of Caution: Don't make the mistake of thinking that a paragraph is coherent only when its sentences are long and complicated. A series of lengthy sentences with burdensome constructions can be just as difficult to read as too many short and choppy sentences. Lengthy sentences are meaningful only when their length and structure add clarity to the ideas that they are uniting. Nevertheless, you may find it useful to look carefully at your paragraphs and see whether you write short, choppy sentences again and again. If you do, then chances are that you can improve your paragraphs by combining some of the sentences to indicate the relationships among your ideas.

SUMMARY

1. By combining brief, simple sentences in longer, more developed sentences, you can render your paragraph more coherent and less choppy.

2. Longer, more developed sentences can more clearly establish the relationships among the facts and ideas in your sentences by emphasizing important points and subordinating less important points.

3. Do not, however, think that a paragraph is coherent only when its sentences are long and complicated: sentence length should reflect the relationships among the ideas being presented.

EXERCISES

I. In each of the following paragraphs, too many sentences are of similar length and structure. Rewrite each paragraph using sentence structures which make the paragraph clearer and easier to follow.

A. Blood pressure is a force. This force is the flow of blood against the walls of the arteries. The pumping action of the heart creates this force. The pressure of the blood rises with each contraction of the heart. The pressure of the blood then falls as the heart relaxes. The blood goes throughout the body. The blood goes by way of a system. This system is a system of vessels. These vessels eventually return the blood to the heart. The movement of blood is rapid. A drop of blood usually requires less than one minute to complete a trip. This trip is from and to the heart.

B. In a span of time European newcomers to the United States uprooted more than half a million Indians. The time span was three hundred years (1600–1900). The European newcomers also conquered the Indians. The Indians were friendly to the newcomers. Of course, this friendliness was naive. The newcomers' power was not foreseen by the Indians. The threat of the newcomers was also not foreseen. However, soon something became apparent. It became apparent that too many whites were beginning to arrive. Friction developed. This friction developed over land. Gradually hatred and fear of Indians grew up among the settlers. These settlers regarded the Indians as savages. The United States won its independence in 1783. By this time most of the tribes along the Atlantic coast had been dispossessed of their land.

C. Land is one of the best investments a person can make. One can do whatever he chooses with his land. He can build the house of his dreams on it. He can use the land as a weekend camping resort. He can cultivate the land. He can landscape it. A piece of land can be a place where one can put down roots. It can be "home." A person can relax on his own land. He can do almost anything there without fear of reprisal. The value of land is on the rise. Land bought today will surely double in value in the next ten years. Land is an investment which can satisfy anyone. It is an investment one should never pass up.

D. A method of testing for fetal abnormalities has been developed. This method is called transabdominal amniocentesis. This method involves drawing amniotic fluid from the mother. Amniotic fluid is located in the uterus. The fluid is drawn for study. Requirements for the process are antiseptic solution, sterile towels, syringe and needle, and a four-inch spinal needle. The syringe and first needle are needed for inserting the local anesthetic. The four-inch spinal needle is employed to penetrate the walls of the uterine cavity. First of all, the uterus is probed. The unobstructed area anterior to the fetal shoulder is located. The selected site for needle entry is then prepared. The site is prepared with antiseptic solution. A local anesthetic may be introduced at this point. It is not always needed. The puncture needle is inserted into the cavity. From the cavity, fluid is removed. This fluid is tested. The procedure takes only a short time. It tells whether or not the fetus is normal or has any congenital abnormalities.

Grammatical Consistency

Ordering support in a natural and effective way, providing devices of transition, and combining choppy sentences into developed sentences with clear connections between thoughts are all important means for achieving coherence. Once the writer has employed these techniques, he can go one step further to ensure that a paragraph is coherent. The writer can check for grammatical consistency or, more specifically, consistent verb tense and consistent pronoun person.

Consistent Verb Tense

Briefly stated, *tense* means time. When you select a verb tense for a single sentence, you consider when the action or state of being that is expressed in the sentence occurs—in the past, in the present, or in the future. Similarly, when you select a predominant verb tense for a paragraph, you consider at what point in time a series of events or ideas exists.

There are three major tenses in English:

Tense	*Example*
1. Present	I look
2. Past	I looked
3. Future	I will look

If you begin a paragraph in one tense, you should stick to that tense throughout the paragraph. You can make exceptions, though, when a given sentence logically requires the use of another tense. For instance, when you recount a past experience as support for a topic sentence, shifting from the present tense into past tense is natural and not disturbing to your reader. Often, however, shifts in verb tense are unnecessary, and you will find that your writing is smoother and more coherent when you remain in one tense. The paragraph below, for instance, shifts back and forth unnecessarily between present, past, and future:

present	Starting college sometimes *results* in a quick weight gain for beginning freshmen. One explanation for this
present (both)	rapid gain in weight *is* the pressure new students *have to*
present	*deal* with. College students *feel* pressure mainly because
future	so much more *will be expected* of them as far as studies
present, future	and grades *are* concerned. Such pressure *will make* stu-
present	dents nervous, and, as a result, they *eat* more food. So-
present	cial pressure also *plays* an important role in weight gain,
	since going to parties to make friends *will increase* their
future	consumption of beer, soda, and snack foods. Another rea-
present	son for weight gain *is* the quality and selection of food in
future	the cafeteria. Many students *will eat* more starches and
past (both)	desserts in the cafeteria than they *did* when they *were* at
	home. In addition to pressure and cafeteria food, lack of
present	exercise *contributes* to weight gain. Instead of developing
future	a regular exercise program, freshmen *will stay* in their
future	rooms and talk or *will sit* in the library and study. As a
present (all)	result, they *do* not *burn* off the extra calories they *take* in.

Had the writer stuck to the present tense instead of weaving back and forth between the present and the future, this paragraph would have been much easier to follow.

Note how much smoother and more effective the same paragraph is when a consistent tense (present) is maintained:

> Starting college sometimes results in a quick weight gain for beginning freshmen. One explanation for this rapid gain in weight is the pressure new students have to deal with. College students feel pressure mainly because so much more is expected of them as far as studies and grades are concerned. Such pressure makes students nervous, and, as a result, they eat more food. Social pressure also plays an important role in weight gain, since going to parties to make friends increases their consumption of beer, soda, and snack foods. Another reason for weight gain is the quality and selection of food in the cafeteria. Many students eat more starches and desserts in the cafeteria than they did when they were at home. In addition to pressure and cafeteria food, lack of exercise contributes to weight gain. Instead of developing a regular exercise program, freshmen stay in their rooms and talk or sit in the library and study. As a result, they do not burn off the extra calories they take in.

All the verbs in this paragraph except two are in the present tense. The exceptions are *did* and *were* in the sentence "Many students eat more starches and desserts in the cafeteria than they did when they were at home." These two verbs *should* logically be in the past tense because the activity they describe occurred *before* the events on which the paragraph focuses—that is, before the freshmen started attending college. In the revised paragraph the verb tenses are both consistent and logical and therefore do not disrupt the flow of ideas and the paragraph's coherence.

SUMMARY

1. There are three major tenses in English: present, past, and future.
2. If you begin writing in one tense, stick to that tense throughout your paragraph unless a given context logically requires the use of a different tense.
3. Illogical and unnecessary shifts in verb tense within a paragraph disrupt the flow of ideas and detract from the paragraph's coherence.

EXERCISES

I. Make the following paragraphs more coherent by eliminating unnecessary shifts in verb tense. For every verb that is in an inappropriate tense, indicate the verb form that would be appropriate.

A. Driving erratically is a characteristic of some drivers. They weave all over the road as if unaware of their actions. On a four-lane road, these drivers will usually drive in two lanes because they are unable to stay in one. On a two-lane road, on the other hand, they drive down the center of the road, not only because they are unable to stay in one lane, but also because they were afraid of hitting the curb at the side of the road. When a car approaches from the opposite direction, they move into their own lane slowly, scaring the other driver half to death. Therefore, careful drivers should be on the alert for erratic drivers who will not always stay in the proper lane.

B. After living in a women's dorm for a little more than one semester, I have noticed that when women come to college they immediately become fanatics. No matter what they looked like, fat or thin, the calorie count of every food item around campus became imprinted on their brains. I am not sure why this fanaticism develops. One possible reason was that living with so many other women made one realize that her own figure might have been less than perfect. Another strong possibility is that calorie counting was an activity that everybody did. Whatever the reason, however, fanaticism about dieting is apparent in every women's dorm on campus.

Consistent Pronoun Person

When you are writing, you should also be consistent in the *person* of the pronouns you use (see pp. 125–126). You may choose, for example, to use the *first-person* pronouns *I* and *we,* or you may prefer to use the *third-person* pronouns *he, she, it, one,* and *they.* On some occasions, you may find it appropriate to use *you,* the *second-person* pronoun. But, whatever pronoun person you choose, you should use it consistently throughout your paragraph.

Whether you use first-person pronouns or third-person pronouns depends, in large measure, on the kind of feeling you wish to generate in your writing. If you wish to create a personal tone, the first-person pronouns *I* and *we* are appropriate, for they convey to the reader the feeling that you, the writer, are speaking for and about yourself. If, on the other hand, you prefer to remain more detached in your presentation of facts and ideas, you should use third-person pronouns because they create distance between you and your audience and imply that you are writing from an objective stance. Because expository paragraphs are paragraphs that *explain,* they are usually written in the third person.

The pronoun *you* is used less frequently in expository writing than the first-person and third-person pronouns. It is reserved primarily for instances where the writer is speaking to a clearly defined audience. Process analysis paragraphs that give instructions, like many of the paragraphs addressed to students in this book, are often written with a direct "you."

The main point to remember about the use of pronouns, however, is that you should remain consistent in the person of your pronouns throughout each paragraph. Mixing the persons of the pronouns in a paragraph, unless there is a clear-cut reason for doing so, usually results in awkward shifts in viewpoint which can destroy the coherence of the paragraph.

Consider, for instance, the following paragraph:

> Everywhere *one* goes and everywhere *one* looks, there are different kinds of signs. Motorists rely on road signs to know when to "stop," "yield," and "detour." Lines on the road let *them* know when it is safe to pass, and speed limit signs tell *them* how fast *they* are permitted to travel. Some signs give *us* helpful information which *we* need to carry out *our* daily activities safely and efficiently. Signs in parks and zoos, for example, tell *us* to "keep off the grass" and ask that *we* "don't feed the animals," and signs where construction is taking place warn *us* about "wet paint" and "falling debris." Signs in airports and shopping centers tell passers-by where *they* can "enter" and "exit" buildings and let *them* know where *they* are allowed to smoke and where *they* are not allowed to smoke. Signs are also an extremely effective way to advertise. Many kinds of businesses advertise their products and services on signs. America is simply cluttered with signs—but how could *we* possibly survive without them?

This paragraph begins with sentences containing both singular and plural third-person pronouns *(one, them, they),* abruptly shifts, toward the middle, to sentences containing first-person pronouns *(us, we, our),* and then moves back and forth between third- and first-person pronouns. The result is that the writer jars the perspective of the reader through a series of abrupt shifts in point of view.

Had the writer been consistent in the person of the pronouns he used, as in the following revised version of the paragraph, he would have maintained a consistent point of view throughout:

> Everywhere people go and everywhere they look, there are different kinds of signs. Motorists rely on road signs to know when to "stop," "yield," and "detour." Lines on the road let *them* know when it is safe to pass, and speed limit signs tell *them* how fast *they* are permitted to travel. Some signs provide helpful information which makes it easier for people to carry out their activities safely and efficiently. Signs in parks and zoos, for example, ask that *they* "keep off the grass" and "don't feed

the animals," and signs where construction is taking place warn about the hazards of "wet paint" and "falling debris." Signs in airports and shopping centers tell passers-by where *they* can "enter" and "exit" buildings and let *them* know where *they* are allowed to smoke and where *they* are not allowed to smoke. Signs also are an extremely effective way to advertise. Many kinds of businesses use signs to advertise their products and services. America is simply cluttered with signs, but much of the information they give makes life safer and simpler for everyone.

In this revised version, the writer has consistently used third-person pronouns, and his paragraph is clearer and more coherent as a result.

One major problem that students frequently encounter when they write paragraphs is the incorrect use of the pronoun *you*. As mentioned earlier in this section, the pronoun *you* should be used only when the writer is speaking directly to a clearly defined audience. Students often make the mistake of using *you* without a definite audience in mind, as in the statement, *"You* have to suffer to be beautiful." They do so because they are accustomed to using the "indefinite *you*," as it is called, in their speech, where informal and colloquial patterns of pronoun usage are permissible. In written language, however, where clarity of expression is necessary, frequent use of the indefinite *you* creates an overly informal tone and sometimes results in confusion for the reader. The more precise third-person pronouns—*he, they, she,* or even the formal-sounding *one*—are usually more appropriate.

The use of the indefinite *you* becomes an especially annoying problem in paragraphs such as the following, in which the writer alternates between *you* and the third-person pronouns *they, their,* and *them:*

> Living on campus is a learning experience. Not only do students grow mentally, but *you* also learn to be independent. Many young people fear moving away from home; *they* fear facing the world alone. But as a result of *their* experiences on campus, *they* become more self-assured. For instance, on campus *you* have to do everything for *yourself,* from laundry to cleaning. And students must decide how much time to devote to studies and how much time to devote to social activities. A party invitation for the night before an exam is a test of *your* acquired self-discipline; turning such invitations down demonstrates that *you* have learned a great deal from *your* experiences on campus. Finally, the greatest learning experience comes from the exposure students gain in the dormitory setting to people from different backgrounds. Tolerance, flexibility, and other traits that will aid *them* in the adult world are generally learned by students who successfully adjust to living on campus.

By shifting from the use of third-person pronouns to the use of the indefinite *you* in observations such as "on campus you have to do everything for yourself," the writer of this paragraph creates an inconsistency in tone and a confusion in point of view. The focus of the paragraph is on "young people" and "students," which are most appropriately referred to as "they." When the pronoun "you" suddenly appears, the reader wonders to whom it refers: students? the reader? people in general? While *you* is often used in conversation as a substitute for *people in general,* it should not be used in this way in expository writing. And it should never be used interchangeably with third-person pronouns in the same paragraph.

Notice how much more clearly the same paragraph reads when the writer sticks to third-person pronouns throughout the paragraph:

> Living on campus is a learning experience. Not only do students grow mentally, but *they* also learn to be independent. Many young people fear moving away from home; *they* fear facing the world alone. But as a result of *their* experiences on campus, *they* become more self-assured. For instance, on campus *they* have to do everything for *themselves,* from laundry to cleaning. And students must decide how much time to devote to studies and how much time to devote to social activities. A party invitation for the night before an exam is a test of *their* acquired self-discipline; turning such invitations down demonstrates that *they* have learned a great deal from *their* experiences on campus. Finally, the greatest learning experience comes from the exposure students gain in the dormitory setting to people from different backgrounds. Tolerance, flexibility, and other traits that will aid *them* in the adult world are generally learned by students who successfully adjust to living on campus.

With the indefinite *you* removed and the person of the pronouns made consistent, the sentences and ideas in this paragraph flow more smoothly, and the paragraph gains coherence.

Remember, then, never use the pronoun *you* in your writing unless you have a definite audience in mind, and never use the indefinite *you* in paragraphs in which third-person pronouns are more appropriate.

SUMMARY

1. Another way to ensure that your paragraphs are coherent is to maintain consistency in the person of the pronouns which you use.
2. Whether you use first-person pronouns or third-person pronouns largely depends on the tone you wish to adopt in a paragraph. First-person pronouns are informal and personal; third-person

pronouns are more distant and objective. Most expository paragraphs are written in the third person.

3. In expository writing, the pronoun *you* is used less frequently than first- and third-person pronouns and is reserved primarily for instances where the writer is speaking to a clearly defined audience.

4. Remain consistent in the person of the pronouns throughout a paragraph. Mixing the persons of the pronouns in a single paragraph, unless there is a clear-cut reason for doing so, results in awkward shifts in perspective which can destroy the coherence of the paragraph.

5. Avoid using the indefinite *you*. Although it may be appropriate in conversations, in written paragraphs the indefinite *you* creates vagueness and an overly casual tone.

EXERCISES

I. Read each of the following paragraphs carefully. Identify any pronouns which are improperly used and indicate the correct pronoun.

A. Final exams are psychologically difficult for students and, with few exceptions, students hate them. They know that finals can make or break your grade, regardless of how well you have done previously in the semester. So students usually cram relentlessly; they bury themselves in notes, texts, and supplementary readings with the hope that something will sink in. Soon, though, the pressure begins taking its toll: you may become discouraged, frustrated, short-tempered, and fatigued. Regardless of whether a student has one or all of these symptoms, he is sure to have the disease: "finalitis."

B. I enjoy using my creative abilities when I teach. I prefer making my own teaching materials, such as educational games, learning centers, drill cards, and exercises. So when funds for professionally made textbooks and workbooks are low and materials are difficult to obtain, my students never suffer. And you find that your materials are better anyway. I also enjoy creating my own bulletin-board materials. Why should you go out and buy snowflakes or Thanksgiving scenes or letters made by a machine when you can make them yourself? My students appreciate the items on the bulletin board more when they realize the effort that I have put into them. And I find that my creative efforts help students to discover the rewards of using their own creative abilities. Can you imagine the satisfaction they feel when they see something they made—a map or a picture—up on the bulletin board? No professionally made materials can instill that sense of accomplishment and pride.

C. Cashiers are expected to handle any situation that may arise in the course of a day's work without becoming disgruntled or unpleasant. For instance, when you buy something, you expect it to be in working order, and if it is not, you become upset. Generally, when the disappointed buyer returns a broken item, he takes out his feelings on the first person he sees. And that person is usually the cashier. Sometimes the dissatisfied customer can be violent, cursing loudly and even threatening physical harm if his demands are not immediately met. You must keep your cool through it all and wait until the emotion has subsided; then you can deal with the problem in an efficient and appropriate fashion. After the merchandise has been returned and a refund has been made, the customer feels embarrassed. All of the apologies in the world, however, cannot make the job of a cashier any easier.

D. A home garden offers an inexpensive and nutritious alternative to paying exorbitant prices for supermarket produce. Green beans, for instance, cost as much as a dollar a pound in the supermarket, but you can grow a year's supply of beans on a small plot of land for only a few cents and a little effort. Apples and oranges, too, can be expensive, especially during off-season months. But if the climate is right, you can plant a fruit tree in your backyard, store the fruit in a cellar or garage, and enjoy fresh fruit all year round at a fraction of the price you would pay for it in a grocery store. In addition to beans and fruit, you can grow tomatoes, squash, peas, potatoes, beets, lettuce, and other types of produce in your garden. The savings to your pocketbook can prove phenomenal: if properly planted and tended, a ten-foot-square plot of land can produce several hundred dollars' worth of produce.

Chapter 6

From Paragraph to Essay

Thus far you have learned how to plan, unify, develop, organize, and order paragraphs. Of course, single, isolated paragraphs are not the most common form in which written work appears. But, because they do serve as building blocks for longer forms of writing, learning how to structure paragraphs effectively represents an important step in mastering the longer forms.

This chapter will teach you how to apply to the short essay the principles you have learned about writing paragraphs. The paragraph is, in essence, an essay in miniature, and what you have learned about concepts like unity and development will be useful to you as you begin to write essays.

The 1-3-1 Essay

One of the most commonly assigned forms of the essay is that consisting of five paragraphs: an *introduction,* three *body paragraphs,* and a *conclusion.* Because of its five-paragraph structure, this type of essay is often called the 1-3-1 essay. The first paragraph in the 1-3-1 essay, the introduction, states the writer's *thesis* in a *thesis sentence* and indicates how the writer will go about developing this thesis. The thesis sentence is the most important sentence in an essay. Like the topic sentence of a paragraph, it expresses a controlling idea (the thesis), which the rest of the essay develops and supports. The three paragraphs which follow the introduction are the body of the essay. Together these paragraphs support and develop the thesis of the essay, in much the same way that the primary supports in a paragraph back up the controlling idea of the paragraph. The final paragraph in the 1-3-1 essay is the conclusion. In it the writer ties together the thoughts presented in the essay and brings the work to a close.

The following essay illustrates the 1-3-1 form:

Thesis
(italicized)

When the famous magician Harry Houdini performed one of his fantastic escape acts, members of the audience invariably experienced a thrill. *Houdini, a successful showman, knew how to captivate his spectators.* He could excite them with the danger and suspense of his acts, amuse them with unexpected touches of humor, or stimulate their curiosity.

Body
paragraph
1

A performance of the "metal trunk act," for example, was certain to convey a sense of danger and suspense to Houdini's onlookers. The act began on a shaky, abandoned suspension bridge at least one hundred feet above a raging river. Hundreds of people gathered along the banks of the river and listened to an announcer standing at the edge of the bridge. Shouting into a megaphone, the announcer described the upcoming act in detail, always emphasizing the element of danger the stunt entailed. Following the announcer's introduction, four members of Houdini's company fitted the artist into a straitjacket, wrapped him in chains, and placed him in an airtight metal trunk. As the crew shut the trunk lid, members of the audience could be heard to murmur, "I can't believe it" and "He'll surely be killed." The crew then took the trunk to the edge of the bridge and hurled it into the swirling water. For ten suspenseful minutes the audience anxiously waited—and then suddenly Houdini rose to the surface of the water, waving his arms victoriously as two members of his company pulled him from the water into a boat.

Body
paragraph
2

While tricks like the "metal trunk act" were intended to create an element of danger, other acts appealed to the audience's sense of humor. The "swinging straitjacket act" was one of these humorous stunts. When the curtain opened, members of the audience began to laugh as they viewed the unexpected sight on the stage. Houdini was hanging upside down above a tankful of mud, suspended from a rope that extended to the ceiling and through a pulley back down to the stage. The presence of a stagehand holding the end of the rope was particularly amusing, for the spectators knew that if the stagehand released the rope Houdini would fall into the slimy mud below. An announcer soon appeared on stage to warn the audience that the stagehand would begin to lower the rope slowly—but that if Houdini could escape from the confines of the straitjacket within thirty seconds, he would be spared the dunk in the mud. As Houdini began to disengage himself from the straitjacket, the stagehand gradually lowered the rope. Inches before reaching the mud, Houdini freed himself from his bonds, smiled at his audience, and shouted, "I made it!" Then, to the surprise of everyone in the audience, the stagehand seemed to let go of the rope accidentally, and Houdini took his mud bath after all. This was a delightful finishing touch, and the crowd responded with a great deal of laughter.

Body
paragraph
3

Stunts like the "glass case act," finally, captivated onlookers by arousing their curiosity. At the beginning of the act, the curtain opened on a stage that was completely empty except for a large glass case filled almost to the brim with water. Members of the audience, not receiving any explanation, stared at the large container for two long minutes. Their curiosity now aroused, they eagerly awaited the coming attraction. Suddenly, Houdini, wearing a bathing suit, walked across the stage. He stopped in front of the glass box and turned quickly to face the spectators, who seemed to be sitting on the edges of their seats as the announcer dramatically described the event that was about to take place. As soon as the announcer finished his introduction, two stagehands bound the escape artist from head to toe with chain and rope, raised him to the top of a stepladder which had been placed beside the glass box, and dropped him headfirst into the water. Curiosity quickly changed to feelings of danger and suspense as most of the onlookers jumped to their feet and some even ran to the edge of the stage. Meanwhile Houdini, during the self-imposed time limit of a minute and a half, struggled to free himself from the chain and rope. When he had accomplished the feat, he quickly swam to the surface to inhale a breath of fresh air and to receive the enthusiastic applause of the audience.

Conclusion

Houdini's performances were successful not only because of his amazing stunts but because of his ingenious use of dramatic devices that kept his audiences enthralled. In some acts he created an atmosphere of suspense and danger that kept his spectators breathless. In other acts he included elements of humor that drew laughter and applause. And in still other acts he appealed to his spectators' sense of curiosity. These dramatic devices were effective in capturing the attention of his audience, holding it while the actual stunts were performed, and keeping Houdini in the spectators' minds even after the performance was over.

In order to clarify the structure of this essay on Houdini, we have diagramed it in Figure 6-1. As the diagram illustrates, the first paragraph of the essay contains the thesis sentence, "Houdini, a successful showman, knew how to captivate his spectators." The paragraph also indicates that the author will support the thesis sentence by giving examples of the ways in which Houdini captivated his audiences, namely through (1) *danger and suspense,* (2) *humor,* and (3) *curiosity.* The three paragraphs in the body of the essay take up these points one by one. The final paragraph brings the essay to a conclusion by restating, in different words, the thesis and the divisions used to support the thesis. Together these sections of the essay illustrate the 1-3-1 form: a *one-* paragraph introduction, *three* body paragraphs, and a *one-*paragraph conclusion.

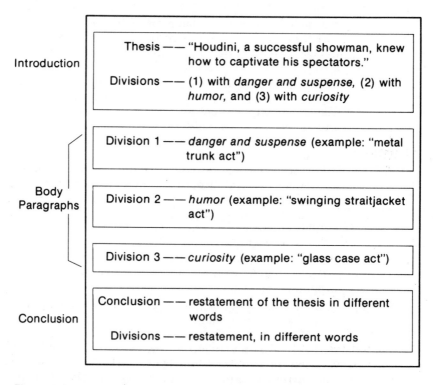

Figure 6-1

Using the 1-3-1 Essay

You may feel, at first, that the 1-3-1 essay is a confining form, one which stifles creativity by putting restrictions on the writer. But keep in mind that there is no hard-and-fast rule that requires you, when writing an essay, to follow the 1-3-1 formula—to use three paragraphs for the body of your essay or, for that matter, only one paragraph for the introduction or conclusion. In fact, two well-developed paragraphs can often support a thesis sentence. And, of course, you may often find that you need more than three body paragraphs to back up your thesis sentence. But the 1-3-1 formula, while it may seem mechanical, has the value of providing you with a skeleton upon which to construct an effectively developed short essay.

You may find it useful to keep in mind, too, that the primary purpose of much of the writing you do in college is simply to learn to write well—to communicate effectively—and to do so you must concentrate on acquiring a number of particular writing skills. Writing practice in one or more selected forms—the paragraph, the essay, the research paper, and so on—will provide you with the opportunity to gain these skills—skills that will serve you well no matter what type of writing you ultimately do, either for pleasure or on the job. Thus, learning the 1-3-1 essay is not an end in itself but rather a beginning, a way to start you on your way to becoming a self-confident, skillful writer.

SUMMARY

1. The "1-3-1" essay form consists of the following elements:
   a. An introductory paragraph stating the writer's thesis in a thesis sentence and indicating how the writer will develop this thesis.
   b. Three body paragraphs that support and develop the thesis sentence according to the divisions presented in the introductory paragraph.
   c. A concluding paragraph which ties together the thoughts presented in the essay and brings it to a close.
2. Because the 1-3-1 form provides the writer with a skeleton on which to construct an effectively developed short essay, mastering this form is an extremely useful way for students to learn how to write essays.

EXERCISES

I. Read the following essay carefully. As you will notice, it follows the 1-3-1 formula. Underline the thesis sentence, and write down the three divisions which constitute the body of the essay. Explain how the final paragraph in the essay functions as a conclusion.

Suicide and Its Causes

It has been said that each of us, at one time or another, considers committing suicide. But the real tragedy is that each year more than half a million people not only contemplate suicide but actually succeed in taking their own lives. This high suicide rate is influenced by a number of factors. Among them are psychological states, sociological conditions, and ineffective means of prevention.

First, various psychological states may lead to suicide. One such state is depression, the most prevalent mental disorder in the world today. Depression itself is often caused by loneliness, loss of a loved one, or feelings of inadequacy. Individuals experiencing depression may be plagued by a sense of hopelessness and helplessness; they may feel that there is nothing they can do to make a real change for the better in their lives. Another psychological state that sometimes leads to suicide is intense guilt—the belief that one has committed such an unforgivable act that one no longer deserves to be alive. A third mental state that often results in suicide—tension—may stem from a variety of causes. Pressure from deadlines, excessive work or family demands, or the unreasonable expectations that, for example, parents may place on their children may produce such severe tension that some individuals are unable to cope with it. One source of tension that is especially noticeable these days is financial insecurity. In the face of inflation and devaluation of the dollar, even the rich are often overcome by anxiety and may end up taking their own lives. The reason? The same that led to so many suicides during the Great Depression—fear of poverty.

Like economic insecurity, many psychological problems are rooted in sociological conditions. In fact, there are several sociological factors—including national or ethnic identity, race, sex, and age—that play a role in the majority of suicides. For instance, the suicide rate in certain societies is high because of ancient traditions that condone suicide as an honorable alternative to hardship. Closer to home, a rapidly expanding technology and an increasingly accelerating life style have resulted in a high incidence of suicide among middle- and upper-class Americans. Until recently, blacks did not experience the particular pressures that the middle class did, but as involvement of blacks in mainstream America increases, they may become more susceptible to suicidal urges. There are also differences in suicide rates among men and women. Women lead men in the category of attempted suicides, but men are apparently more successful when they do try. Their success is probably due to their ability to get their hands on lethal weapons more easily. While few children commit suicide, the rate of attempts among adolescents is steadily rising. Broken homes and the increased availability of drugs and alcohol are undoubtedly the cause. Among adults, suicide attempts at middle age are most common; at the midpoint in one's life, escape from past failures often seems attractive. Those who survive middle age, however, are less likely to attempt to take their lives. With age comes, it seems, the ability to accept the stresses and disappointments of life.

Finally, the last and perhaps most perplexing factor contributing to the high suicide rate is the ineffectiveness of present means of suicide prevention. Suicide prevention is difficult for several reasons. First of all, it is evident that in order for suicide to be prevented, the troubled individual must seek help. Many people never seek aid, and those who might be able to help never have the chance to do so. Even when a person contemplating suicide does call a hotline or a friend, he may be so emotionally overwrought that he cannot tell the person on the phone where he is, even if he wants to. And the problem does not end when one suicide attempt is prevented because there is no assurance that another attempt won't be made. In many cases, a person who has tried once eventually tries again. The problems he sought to escape are still there when he returns to daily life, so it is not surprising that he may try to escape them again.

A better understanding of the main factors contributing to the high suicide rate, including psychological states, sociological factors, and ineffective means of prevention, is vitally necessary in our society. Perhaps as we become more aware of suicide as a growing problem and more knowledgeable about its contributing factors, we will be able to do more to prevent the tragedy of suicide.

Writing the Essay

There are two basic ways to go about writing a 1-3-1 expository essay. The first is to expand a general-to-specific paragraph which you have written into an essay. The second is the more direct procedure of simply writing an essay from scratch. In the remainder of this chapter we'll show you how to write essays using both methods.

Paragraph into Essay

As we mentioned earlier in this chapter, a paragraph is an essay in miniature. Each of the paragraphs in the body of an essay supports the thesis sentence in the introductory paragraph of the essay in the same way that each of the primary supports in a paragraph backs up the topic sentence. To turn a paragraph into an essay, you follow a relatively simple procedure involving *five* basic steps:

1. Make the topic sentence of the paragraph the thesis sentence of the essay.
2. Use each of the primary supports in the paragraph as the topic sentence of each of the body paragraphs in the essay.
3. Write the body paragraphs of the essay.
4. Supply an introductory paragraph.
5. Supply a concluding paragraph.

To understand how the procedure works, you may find it helpful to examine the diagram in Figure 6-2. As the diagram indicates, the topic sentence of the paragraph becomes the thesis sentence in the introductory paragraph of the essay, and each of the primary supports in the original paragraph furnishes a topic sentence for a body paragraph in the essay. By completing the body paragraphs and then supplying an introductory paragraph and a concluding paragraph, the writer can construct an essay by expanding the ideas in the paragraph.

Consider, for example, the following paragraph as potential material for a 1-3-1 essay:

> The German countryside offers visitors a number of enchanting sights. Travelers to the mountainous regions, for example, are struck by both the beauty of the landscape and the richness of the area's historical heritage. Majestic snowcaps rise above dense forests and deep blue lakes of cold, clear water. Scattered throughout the mountains are medieval castles that sightseers are welcome to explore. Visitors may also tour the picturesque villages that dot the valleys. A yearly attraction that draws many tourists to rural Germany is the May Day celebration. Each village has its own colorful festival of dancing and feasting. Dressed in medieval costumes especially made for the celebration, the villagers dance through the streets like characters in a book of fairy tales. The deep forests, too, resemble scenes from fairy-tale books. Trickling streams, luxuriant undergrowth, and purple violets growing amid dark green moss give the forests a dreamlike quality. And sightseers may still come across the proverbial woodsman who kindly watches over anyone who ventures through the forest.

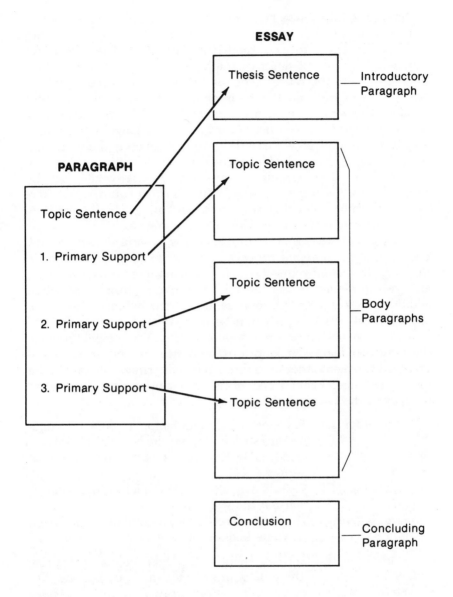

Figure 6-2

By following the steps for converting a paragraph into an essay, the writer can construct an essay from this paragraph on the German countryside.

Step 1: *Take the topic sentence from the paragraph and use it as the thesis sentence of the essay.* Most topic sentences can function as thesis sentences because both topic sentences and thesis sentences introduce a topic, both make a statement about the topic, and both become the central focus of the writer's attention. They are, as we stated earlier in discussing paragraphs, a contract which the writer establishes with the reader. The difference between the topic sentence of a paragraph and the thesis sentence of an essay is the amount of space the writer has at his disposal for making his point. In a paragraph, for example, the writer must drive home a controlling idea in a few hundred words or less, while in an essay the writer has several paragraphs in which to develop a thesis. Thus, in constructing an essay from the paragraph on Germany, the writer would begin by simply taking the topic sentence, "The German countryside offers visitors a number of enchanting sights," and using it in the introductory paragraph of the essay as the thesis sentence.

Step 2: *Take the primary supports in the paragraph and use each one as the topic sentence for each of the three body paragraphs in the essay.* If you find yourself with fewer than three primary supports and wish to remain within the 1-3-1 formula, you can construct an additional body-paragraph topic sentence that supports and develops the thesis sentence; if you have more than three primary supports, you can select the three supports which you feel will provide the most convincing back-up for the thesis sentence. In the paragraph on Germany, there are three points of primary support, each dealing with a different aspect of the "enchanting sights" there are to enjoy in the German countryside:

Primary Support 1: Travelers to the mountainous regions, for example, are struck both by the beauty of the landscape and by the richness of the area's historical heritage.

Primary Support 2: Visitors may also tour the picturesque villages that dot the valleys.

Primary Support 3: The deep forests, too, resemble scenes from fairy-tale books.

In an essay on the German countryside, these points of primary support will serve as the topic sentences for the body paragraphs.

Step 3: *Write a paragraph developing each point of primary support.* These three paragraphs will be the body paragraphs in the essay. To carry out this step, follow the procedure you learned for writing paragraphs: select primary supports for the controlling idea of each paragraph, back up the primary supports with secondary supports, choose a suitable method of development, and organize your material to give the paragraph coherence.

In constructing the *primary* supports for the topic sentence of each body paragraph, you may find that you can use facts and ideas that served as *secondary* supports in the original paragraph. You may, however, have to furnish additional primary support—just as you may have to supply a topic sentence for one of the body paragraphs of the essay. In the first body paragraph of the essay on the German countryside, for instance, the writer used two secondary supports from the original paragraph as primary supports: *snowcaps* and *castles.* But he has added a third: *waterfalls.* Moreover, the writer has provided, for his *secondary* support, some information that did not appear in the original paragraph. You may notice, too, that he has made other changes—he's turned the "snowcap" sentence of the original paragraph into two sentences in the body paragraph. You will probably find, as he did, that because more room is available in the essay than in the paragraph, you'll want to supply more supporting material and revise some of your sentences to fit the essay format.

Finally, for the sake of overall coherence, it may often be necessary to add transitional material at the end of a body paragraph to smooth your reader's way between paragraphs—just as within a paragraph you use transitional devices to enable your reader to move easily from one idea to the next or from one sentence to the next. Always keep in mind, however, that the function of the body paragraphs is to support the thesis of the essay. Transitional devices that are too long or too elaborate may distract your reader from the essay's central idea and undermine the unity and coherence of the essay. A single transitional sentence, or even a transitional word or phrase, is usually enough to prepare your reader for the topic sentence of the next paragraph.

The author of the German countryside paragraph wrote the following three body paragraphs for his essay:

Body Paragraph 1:

Topic sentence   *Travelers to the mountain regions are struck by both the beauty of the landscape and the richness of the area's historical heritage.* In these regions travelers can view snowcaps even in the springtime. The snowcapped mountains rise majestically above dense forests and deep blue lakes filled with cold, clear water. The loveliest in Germany, these lakes are basins that were originally carved out by glaciers. Their water is so pure that fish can be seen swimming at the bottom. Adding to the natural beauty of the mountain regions are the waterfalls that seem to leap from the mountainsides, draining the clear pools and plunging down long ledges into swirling currents below. Man has added beauty to the landscape through the centuries by building marvelous castles which are interesting to explore, castles which tourists love to visit and let their imaginations run

Transition	wild over. *When visitors tire of the mountains, they can find delight in the valleys.*
	Body Paragraph 2:
Topic sentence	The valleys harbor picturesque villages that are centers of activity. Surrounding the villages and ranging out to the feet of the mountains are neatly cultivated patches of farmland. As visitors pass through the farmland and near a village, they may well recall pictures of villages they have seen in books of fairy tales. Each village is crowded with houses lining the cobblestone streets. These houses have window boxes or flower beds filled with colorful tulips and pansies. In the center of each village stands a stone church with a bell hanging in its steeple. Every year many tourists come to rural Germany for the May Day celebration. Given in honor of spring, the May Day celebration in each village is a colorful festival of dancing and feasting. Villagers dress in medieval costumes and erect a maypole in the town square for the costumed girls to dance around. The maypole is adorned with flowers and strands of brightly colored material. Not only do the villagers deck themselves out with bright colors, but they decorate their homes as well. And in small prayer stands located on the slopes outside the villages, they place flowers in honor of the new season. Natural beauty is adorned further, and the overall result is a charm that few
Transition	countries can rival. *The valley villages, though, are not the only places in Germany that possess the mystical charms that visitors have come to associate with that country.*
	Body Paragraph 3:
Topic sentence	*The deep forests, too, resemble scenes from fairy-tale books.* Trickling streams, luxuriant undergrowth, and purple violets growing amid dark green moss enhance the dreamlike quality of the forests. Nature trails wind through these dark, mysterious woods, and there are benches where visitors can stop to rest or take in the scenery. Many of the animals inhabiting the forests are very tame, and in the autumn, when the blueberry bushes are heavy with dark, delicious berries, visitors pick the berries to feed to the squirrels and the deer. When blueberries are not in season, deer can be seen close by nibbling at fir or white birch trees. And visitors may still encounter the proverbial woodsman who watches with kindness anyone who ventures into the forests.

Each of these paragraphs develops its topic sentence in full. Body paragraphs 1 and 2 contain transitional sentences which lead the reader into the next paragraph. Together the paragraphs support the essay's thesis that "the German countryside offers visitors a number of enchanting sights."

Step 4: *Write an introductory paragraph for the essay.* Once you have completed the body paragraphs and furnished necessary transition, you are ready to write an introductory paragraph to the essay. In writing such a paragraph, keep in mind that the introduction to an essay should accomplish three things:

1. capture the reader's interest
2. state the thesis
3. introduce the divisions in the body paragraphs

While there is no hard-and-fast rule to follow when you write an introductory paragraph, most introductions begin by attracting the reader's interest, *then* go on to state the thesis and introduce the divisions to be discussed in the body paragraphs.

The following diagram illustrates the structure which introductory paragraphs usually follow:

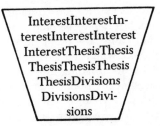

As the diagram indicates, the writer starts out by getting the reader involved in the topic of the essay. After capturing the interest of the reader, the writer states the thesis and gives the reader an idea of the kinds of support which the body paragraphs will provide.

How does a writer succeed in capturing the attention of a reader? Or, put another way, how does a writer convince a reader that the essay to come will be informative, interesting, entertaining, or otherwise worth reading? There are a number of well-established devices a writer can use to stimulate reader interest. For the essay on Houdini, for instance, there are many possible "lead-ins," each involving a different interest-catching technique. The introduction of the essay, as it appears at the beginning of this chapter, employs *a simple, well-focused generalization:*

> When the famous magician Harry Houdini performed one of his fantastic escape acts, members of the audience invariably experienced a thrill. *Houdini, a successful showman, knew how to captivate his spectators.* He could excite them with the danger and suspense of his acts, amuse them with unexpected touches of humor, or stimulate their curiosity.

Other methods that could be used to introduce the Houdini essay are these:

1. *Personal testimony*

Reading the biography of the great escape artist Harry Houdini has been an enlightening experience for me. Although the book has made me admire the Great Houdini and his amazing feats even more than I did before, it has shown me that only half of Houdini's performance was magic. The other half was showmanship. *Houdini, a successful showman, knew how to captivate his spectators.* He could excite them with the danger and suspense of his acts, amuse them with unexpected touches of humor, or stimulate their curiosity.

2. *Anecdote*

Harry Houdini, the great escape artist, never ran out of ways to attract the interest of the general public. Even the events surrounding his death demonstrate his flair for the dramatic. According to an often quoted story, Houdini, just before he died, told his wife that he would communicate with her from "the other side." From his death to just before her death in 1943, when she gave up trying to reach him, this promise kept his widow from fading into obscurity. It was this ability to stimulate the interest of the public that also served him well in life, particularly during his performances. *Houdini, a successful showman, knew how to captivate his spectators.* He could excite them with the danger and suspense of his acts, amuse them with unexpected touches of humor, or stimulate their curiosity.

3. *Factual data*

Harry Houdini, the great escape artist, was born in 1874. There has been some controversy over where he was born. Some biographers argue Budapest, Hungary; others, however, support his claim of having been born in Appleton, Wisconsin. This controversy notwithstanding, Houdini's real name was Erich Weiss, and at an early age Erich demonstrated an uncanny grasp of the art of trapeze flying. As he grew older, he became fascinated with magic and with the fantastic tricks of such performers as the French magician Robert-Houdin, from whose name he later derived Houdini. It was from such magicians that he also gained his showmanship. *Houdini, a successful showman, knew how to captivate his spectators.* He could excite them with the danger and suspense of his acts, amuse them with unexpected touches of humor, or stimulate their curiosity.

4. *Quotation*

In his article on "conjuring" in the 1926 *Encyclopaedia Britannica,* the great master of escape Harry Houdini asserted that he owed his success to his "great physical strength and the fact that he [was] slightly bowlegged." But when one reads about the remarkable career of this amazing performer, one finds the man's showmanship more impressive than his athletic attributes. *Houdini, a successful showman, knew how to captivate his spectators.* He could excite them with the danger and suspense of his acts, amuse them with unexpected touches of humor, or stimulate their curiosity.

5. *A combination of devices*

Born in 1874, the great escape artist Harry Houdini	Factual detail
lived in an age that, as a result of new advances in	
science, was fascinated with the unusual and inex-	Generalization
plicable. The Great Houdini took advantage of his	
audience's taste, performing seemingly impossible	Generalization
tasks and reaping their wonder and appreciation. If	
his audiences only had known that most of what	Generalization
they saw during a performance was easily accom-	
plishable for a "slightly bowlegged" man of "great	Quotation
physical strength," they might not have been quite	
so impressed. *Houdini, however, was a successful*	
showman who knew how to captivate his spectators.	
He could excite them with the danger and suspense	
of his acts, amuse them with unexpected touches of	
humor, or stimulate their curiosity.	

To introduce the essay on Germany, any of the devices we've considered might serve as a means of gaining the reader's interest. In the following paragraph, for example, the writer attracts the reader's attention through a combination of generalization and factual data:

Interest	Close to eight million tourists visit Germany each year. But for many the cities are not the side of Germany that proves most inviting. It is the countryside that they have read about, and
Thesis	it is the countryside that they visit. Indeed, *The German countryside offers visitors a number of enchanting sights.* Among
Divisions	the attractions that visitors flock to see are the mountain regions, the valleys where the villages are situated, and the storybook forests.

Step 5: *Write a concluding paragraph for the essay.* Once you have completed the introduction, you should carefully reread the four paragraphs you have written and prepare to write a concluding paragraph that will accomplish the following:

1. restate the thesis and divisions of the essay (in different words)
2. bring the essay to an end smoothly, without digressing into any new issues

In its most basic form, the concluding paragraph may consist of a brief summary of what has been said in the essay. At first you may find this approach the easiest to use. Such a concluding paragraph should simply restate the thesis and the divisions of the essay, using different wording from that which you used in the introductory paragraph. The essay on Houdini, for example, closes with this paragraph:

> Houdini's performances were successful not only because of his amazing stunts but because of his ingenious use of dramatic devices that kept his audiences enthralled. In some acts he created an atmosphere of suspense and danger that kept his spectators breathless. In other acts he included elements of humor that drew laughter and applause. And in still other acts he appealed to his spectators' sense of curiosity. These dramatic devices were effective in capturing the attention of his audiences, holding it while the actual stunts were performed, and keeping Houdini in the spectators' minds even after the performance was over.

As you become more comfortable writing essays, you can vary the form of your concluding paragraphs. A concluding paragraph should always summarize your main ideas by restating the essay's thesis and divisions in different words. But, in addition, you can use other techniques to bring your essay to a smooth and interesting close. You can, for example:

1. Refer to a particular fact, idea, or quotation that you presented in the introduction, as a means of tying the beginning and the end of your essay together:

> Houdini was therefore not being totally candid when he asserted that he owed his success to his strength and bowleggedness. Certainly he also owed a great deal of his wide acclaim to the fact that he was a splendid showman. As a performer, Houdini achieved great feats by exciting his audience with the elements of danger and suspense, amusing them with humorous antics, and arousing their curiosity.

2. Make a prediction after you have restated the thesis and divisions:

> . . . Had Houdini been just another escape artist, his name might soon have been forgotten. But because he added the qualities of a skillful showman to those of a daring performer, Houdini will probably always be remembered.

3. Make a recommendation after you have restated the thesis and divisions:

> . . . When it comes to showmanship, a budding performer would do well to model his or her techniques after those of the Great Houdini.

As a conclusion to the essay on Germany, the following paragraph is effective because it restates the thesis and divisions presented in the introductory paragraph (page 161), and, in its focus on the tourists who visit Germany, refers to the factual data and generalization in that paragraph:

Restatement of thesis and divisions	Germany, then, can be said to have one of the most beautiful countrysides in the world. Its majestic mountain regions, charming villages nestled in picturesque valleys, and fairy-tale forests are a tourist's delight. It is thus no wonder that such a large percentage of the thousands of people who visit Germany each year head for the country, there to take in sights rarely equaled elsewhere.
Reference to point in introduction	

As a result, the essay is brought to a graceful and logical conclusion, and the reader is left with the feeling that the writer has accomplished what he set out to do.

Once you have completed the five steps, you have succeeded in constructing a 1-3-1 essay from a paragraph, and you are now ready to combine the parts. The complete essay would read as follows:

The German Countryside

Close to eight million tourists visit Germany each year. But for many the cities are not the side of Germany that proves most inviting. It is the countryside that they have read about, and it is the countryside that they visit. Indeed, the German countryside offers visitors a number of enchanting sights. Among the attractions that visitors flock to see are the mountain regions, the valleys where the villages are situated, and the storybook forests.

Travelers to the mountain regions are struck by both the beauty of the landscape and the richness of the area's historical heritage. In these regions travelers can view snowcaps even in the springtime. The snowcapped mountains rise majestically above dense forests and deep blue lakes filled with cold, clear water. The loveliest in Germany, these lakes are basins that were originally carved out by glaciers. Their water is so pure that fish can be seen swimming at the bottom. Adding to the natural beauty of the mountain regions are the waterfalls that seem to leap from the mountainsides, draining the clear pools and plunging down long ledges into swirling currents below. Man has added beauty to the landscape through the centuries by building marvelous castles which are interesting to explore, castles which tourists love to visit and let their imaginations run wild over. When visitors tire of the mountains, they can find delight in the valleys.

The valleys harbor picturesque villages that are centers of activity. Surrounding the villages and ranging out to the feet of the mountains are neatly cultivated patches of farmland. As visitors pass through the farmland and near a village, they may well recall pictures of villages they have seen in books of fairy tales. Each village is crowded with houses that line the cobblestone streets. These houses have window boxes or flower beds filled with colorful tulips and pansies. In the center of each village stands a stone church with a bell hanging in its steeple. Every year many tourists come to rural Germany for the May Day celebration. Given in honor of spring, the May Day celebration in each village is a colorful festival of dancing and feasting. Villagers dress in medieval costumes and erect a maypole in the town square for the costumed girls to dance around. The maypole is adorned with flowers and strands of brightly colored material. Not only do the villagers deck themselves out with bright colors, but they decorate their homes as well. And in small prayer stands located on the slopes outside the villages, they place flowers in honor of the new season. Natural beauty is adorned further, and the overall result is a charm that few countries can rival. The valley villages, though, are not the only places in Germany that possess the mystical charms that visitors have come to associate with that country.

The deep forests, too, resemble scenes out of fairy-tale books. Trickling streams, luxuriant undergrowth, and purple violets growing amid dark green moss enhance the dreamlike quality of the forests. Nature trails wind through these dark, mysterious woods, and there are benches where the visitor can stop to rest or take in the scenery. Many of the animals inhabiting the forests are very tame, and in the autumn, when the blueberry bushes are heavy with dark, delicious berries, visitors pick the berries to feed to the squirrels and the deer. When the blueberries are not in season, deer can be seen close by nibbling at fir or white birch trees. And visitors may still encounter the proverbial woodsman who watches with kindness anyone who ventures into the forests.

Germany, then, can be said to have one of the most beautiful countrysides in the world. Its majestic mountain regions, charming villages nestled in picturesque valleys, and fairy-tale forests are a virtual tourist's delight. It is thus no wonder that such a large percentage of the thousands of people who visit Germany each year head for the country, there to take in sights rarely equaled elsewhere.

SUMMARY

1. There are two basic ways to go about writing 1-3-1 expository essays. The first is to expand a general-to-specific paragraph into an essay. The second is the more direct procedure of simply writing an essay from scratch.

2. To turn a paragraph into an essay, follow these five basic steps:

   a. Make the topic sentence of the paragraph the thesis sentence of the essay.

    b. Make the primary supports in the paragraph the topic sentences for the body paragraphs of the essay.

    c. Write the body paragraphs of the essay.

    d. Supply an introductory paragraph for the essay.

    e. Furnish a concluding paragraph for the essay.

3. When turning a paragraph into an essay, you will find that the secondary supports in the original paragraph can often be used as primary supports in the body paragraphs of the essay.

4. The introductory paragraph of an essay should accomplish three objectives. It should (1) capture the reader's interest, (2) state the thesis of the essay, and (3) introduce the divisions in the body paragraphs of the essay.

5. There are several devices that you can use in an introductory paragraph to capture the interest of your reader. You may use (1) a personal testimony, (2) an anecdote, (3) a simple but well-focused generalization, (4) factual data, (5) a quotation, and (6) a combination of these devices.

6. The concluding paragraph of a 1-3-1 essay should accomplish two main objectives: It should (1) restate the thesis and the divisions of the essay using words different from those in the introductory paragraph and (2) bring the essay to an end smoothly, without digressing into any new issues.

7. There are several devices you can use to write effective concluding paragraphs for your essays. You can (1) refer to a fact, idea, or quotation that you presented in the introduction, as a means of tying the beginning and conclusion of the essay together, (2) make a prediction after you have repeated the thesis and divisions, and (3) make a recommendation after you have repeated the thesis and divisions.

EXERCISES

I. Furnish an introductory paragraph and a concluding paragraph for the following three body paragraphs. To help you get started, we have provided the thesis sentence. When you are finished, you will have a complete 1-3-1 essay.

Thesis Sentence: Winter temperatures need not be uncomfortable if one learns to dress properly.

Body Paragraph 1   Layering, or putting on two light garments instead of one heavy one, is the first way to dress properly for winter temperatures. It is not the *thickness* of a garment that keeps one warm but rather the garment's ability to trap air in its fibers; the air remains enclosed and is eventually warmed to the body's temperature. And layering garments on top of each other traps air between garments as well as within the garments themselves. Of course, some fibers trap more air than others, and garments made with such fibers naturally provide the best source of layering. Goose down, for example, is an excellent insulator because the feathers fluff up to two or three times their size, filling the spaces between them with warm air. Other effective insulators are duck down, polyester, wool, and cotton, in that order. Polyester and wool have the added advantage of providing insulation even when they are wet.

Body Paragraph 2

Wearing a hat and a vest is another way to protect against the cold. Most of the warm air in the body escapes through the top of the head and from the trunk (chest and abdomen). These areas of the body are vitally involved in maintaining warmth because the organs which they contain are the source of body heat. The extremities—legs, arms, toes, and fingers— do not produce heat themselves; they are warmed by the heat which circulates through the body. A protective hat and a vest prevent heat from escaping from the head and the trunk and thus enable the bloodstream to distribute more heat to the extremities.

Body Paragraph 3

If clothing is properly layered and one is wearing a hat and a vest, the best way to keep the extremities from feeling the cold is to keep them moving and to insulate them with gloves and socks. By moving the fingers and toes, one forces blood to circulate through them, and, as was noted, circulation keeps them warm. Wearing gloves and mittens should prevent the warmth of the blood from escaping through the hands. And mittens, because they allow the fingers to warm each other by contact, are more effective than gloves. Wool socks are an excellent way to keep the toes warm because wool resists water, and feet tend to get wet if snow and slush are on the ground. For added insulation, moreover, mittens and socks can themselves be layered in the same way that coats and other garments are.

II. Expand one of the following paragraphs into an essay. Be sure that the paragraph you choose is on a topic which you know enough about to discuss effectively in an essay.

Model: (paragraph)

Life insurance comes in three basic forms. The most common type of life insurance is called *ordinary* life insurance. An ordinary life policy states that premiums are payable for a designated number of years and that the person insured is protected for the face amount of the policy. Ordinary life insurance also guarantees its cash value and provides great flexibility to the owner. *Term* life is the second type of life insurance. Under a term insurance policy, premiums are payable for a specified period of time, and the insured person is covered for the amount stated in the contract. Because term insurance builds no equity or residual value, it is usually the least expensive form of insurance. The third kind of life insurance is *endowment* insurance. An endowment policy also requires that premiums be paid during the maturity period, while the insured person is protected for the face value of the contract. In addition to being covered for the face amount of the policy during its term, the insured receives, at the point when the policy matures, the face value plus interest.

Model: (essay)

Mention life insurance to most people, and they confess they are confused about the subject. People need not be confused, however, because there are actually only three basic types of life insurance—ordinary life, term life, and endowment life—and each has features designed to meet particular requirements.

The most frequently purchased type of life insurance is called *ordinary life insurance.* Ordinary life insurance has two features in common with term and endowment policies: a specified number of years during which the premiums are payable and a specified amount of coverage to be paid when the policyholder dies. It is probably the flexibility of ordinary life insurance, combined with low-cost premiums, that makes it the most popular type. Under an ordinary life insurance policy, premiums are usually payable until the policyholder reaches the age of ninety; thus, the cost of the insurance is spread out over a long period of time. Moreover, premiums can be discontinued by the policyholder prior to age ninety. If they are stopped, the accumulated cash value can be used to buy a fully paid-up life insurance policy. And while an ordinary life insurance policy provides benefits at the time of the policyholder's death, it also accumulates cash value while the policyholder lives (cash value is available under endowment life as well, but at greater cost). The cash value can be borrowed from the policy, or it can be left in the policy to accumulate until the policyholder retires; at that time, it can supplement other retirement income. The features of ordinary life insurance make it flexible enough to suit the needs of many people; some individuals, however, have special needs which require other types.

Term life is the second type of life insurance. Like ordinary life, it has a specified amount of death coverage and a specified number of years during which premiums are payable. Although term life is not as flexible as ordinary life, it also is popular, for two reasons. First, it is the least expensive form of insurance. Since no cash value accumulates during the life of the policy, the cost to the policyholder is just for life insurance. Second, many people purchase term insurance to protect themselves in case of major debt. In particular, people who buy homes secured by a mortgage or business executives who borrow large sums of money may buy term insurance because the period of the insurance can be coordinated to provide coverage if the policyholder dies before the mortgage or the loan is repaid. Although term insurance is attractive because of its relatively low cost and its debt protection, there are occasions when the third type, *endowment* insurance, is the most desirable to buy.

Like the two other kinds of insurance, endowment provides a specified number of years during which premiums are to be paid and a specified amount of death coverage. And, like ordinary life insurance, endowment insurance accumulates cash value. What distinguishes endowment insurance from the other two types is, first, that it works like a savings account. Because it represents a harbor for savings, endowment life is frequently purchased on young children in order to provide cash to pay for their college education. Second, the cost for endowment policies is generally higher than for ordinary or term policies because endowment premiums are payable over a shorter period of time and their cash value is greater. It is easy to understand why endowment policy is a plan that appeals especially to people who can commit themselves to saving money.

Many people never fully understand life insurance. The fact that there are only three basic types of such insurance should make the subject less confusing—particularly because each of the types has distinguishing characteristics. Ordinary life combines death protection and cash value with a low premium. Term life provides death protection and no cash value, but it is the least expensive. Endowment provides death protection, savings facilities, and higher cash value, but it is the most expensive of the three.

A. Living in a dormitory, with many other students as my too-close neighbors, has been enough to try my nerves. First of all, I have had no real privacy or solitude since I moved into the dorm. People are constantly bursting into my room to ask a question or just to chat. I cannot turn them away because I do not want to be rude or unfriendly. Second, at least once a day—and sometimes more often—I have to stand in a long line to wait for something I need. The washers and dryers are always taken, and the showers seem to be in greatest demand whenever I am in the biggest hurry. By far the most irritating aspect of dorm life, however, is the noise. I find it almost impossible to concentrate when music is blaring so loudly that the walls shake. And it is certainly difficult to get enough sleep with all the yelling and screaming I can hear through the building's paper-thin walls. Perhaps a happy medium could be reached, and the dormitory could become a more comfortable place to live—and study—if my neighbors acted with a little more consideration and I exercised a little more patience.

B. According to Christian philosophy, there are three kinds of love which humans may experience. The first type of love is known as *eros.* The word is the name of the Greek god of love and has come to imply a self-seeking love; it usually denotes sexual pleasure without emotional attachment. According to the Bible, Christians who engage in eros are sinful. The second type of love is called *phileo,* a Greek word meaning brotherly love. Phileo is not frowned upon in the Bible, but it is not the love which Christians are ultimately expected to achieve. The most perfect form of Christian love is *agape.* Agape, involving unconditional trust on the part of the lover for the beloved, is the type of love which Christians are taught to seek in their relationships with other people.

C. Regardless of the time of day or of the station, most television game shows follow a predictable format. First of all, every game show has a host. At the beginning of the show, the host jogs to center stage, asks for a round of applause, and smiles at the audience. The host is usually dressed in the latest fashion: male hosts wear well-cut suits, and female hosts wear stylish dresses. When explaining the rules of the game, the host frequently speaks in a rapid manner, using the catchy language of a radio disc jockey. Most game shows feature a guest star or two. Such a "star" is frequently an out-of-work actor or actress whose big series was canceled two or three years ago and whom no one has heard of since. Like the host, the stars are dressed stylishly, and—also like the host—they have the ability to smile nonstop for an entire program. Finally, there is the contestant. Favorite contestants are women who easily become hysterical and men whose hair and pants are unstylishly short and who readily lose their composure at the sight of a female star. Whichever category the contestant falls into, he or she has considerable trouble deciding which prizes to keep and which to give away. Because game shows resemble one another so closely, viewers can't help but wonder where producers find the endless stream of predictable hosts, guest stars, and contestants who people the game-show airwaves.

D. Although high-school sports may not be important to everyone, most students who participate in them are favorably affected by the experience. One major advantage which students receive is the self-confidence they develop from performing before a crowd. This self-confidence contributes to the building of a positive self-image, which adults need in order to function effectively in society. Another benefit to be derived from participation in high-school sports is the friendship which students form with the other players. Because they must cooperate with one another as a team, students learn to deal with and accept the idiosyncracies of others. As a result, they develop a tolerance that should help them relate to people in later life. High-school sports also teach students the importance of discipline and determination. Participating in high-school sports may not prepare students for all the hurdles they may face in life, but it certainly gives them a healthy head start.

III. Expand an expository paragraph that you have written into a 1-3-1 essay.

Writing an Essay from Scratch

If you understand the format of the 1-3-1 essay and can effectively expand a paragraph into such an essay, you should have little trouble learning, in this section, how to write a 1-3-1 essay from scratch—that is, without first developing a paragraph. As in the technique of moving from paragraph to essay, there are certain steps to follow in writing an essay from scratch. These steps are as follows: (1) select a topic, (2) write a thesis sentence, (3) organize the essay, (4) write the topic sentences for the body paragraphs of the essay, and (5) write the body paragraphs of the essay and supply an introduction and a conclusion. The remainder of this chapter will show you how to write an essay by following these five steps.

Step 1: *Select a topic.* In deciding upon a topic for a 1-3-1 essay, you should follow much the same approach you employed when you selected a topic for a paragraph (see pages 9–12). If the selection of topic is up to you, the topic you choose should be one you know enough about—from personal experience, classwork, reading, the media, and so on—to write about with confidence for several hundred words. If, on the other hand, your instructor assigns a topic, you must think carefully about the topic you have been given. Usually, assignments are given in terms of general subject areas (for example, *people, pets, college, travel, books,* and so forth), and your instructor will expect you to narrow the subject area down to a more specific topic which you can handle well.

In narrowing a broad subject area, think of aspects of it with which you are familiar and about which you can write with authority. For instance, in limiting the subject area *people,* you can probably come up with several aspects which would make a good essay: *parents, roommates, customers, sex symbols, adolescents, infants, diplomats, entertainers,* or *high-school coaches.*

If you feel that these topics are still too general, choose one and narrow it down even further. The topic *sex symbols,* for example, might be narrowed to *types of sex symbols, the differences between European and American sex symbols,* or an individual sex symbol such as *Burt Reynolds, Marilyn Monroe,* or *Farrah Fawcett.* Under *entertainers,* to take another example, you might list *country and western singers, disco groups,* or your *favorite vocal soloist.* A narrowing down of the topic *customers,* to take a third example, might produce a number of more specific topics: *customers in fast-food restaurants, hotel customers,* or *the type of customer you least care to deal with on your job.*

Step 2: *Write a thesis sentence for your essay.* Once you have selected a topic, write a thesis sentence about the topic. As we stated earlier in this chapter, the thesis sentence, like the topic sentence of a paragraph, indicates a topic and expresses a controlling idea, which the rest of the essay will develop and support (see pages 147–148). The controlling idea should be broad enough to develop within the framework of a 1-3-1 essay. It should not be so broad or so general, however, that a discussion of it will become vague and meaningless. Nor should the controlling idea be so specific that you find yourself unable to develop it when you begin to write the body paragraphs of your essay.

Thus, if you were writing an essay on the topic of *customers who frequent fast-food restaurants,* you would find that the sentence

> Of the different types of customers who frequent fast-food restaurants, some are more welcome than others.

would make a better thesis sentence than the sentence

> The different types of customers who frequent fast-food restaurants are interesting.

or the sentence

> Of the different types of customers who frequent fast-food restaurants, most enjoy eating hamburgers and French fries.

The first sentence makes an effective thesis sentence because the controlling idea, that some of the customers who visit fast-food restaurants are *more welcome than others,* is a statement which is easier to develop than the more general idea that customers who frequent fast-food restaurants are *interesting* or the flat statement of fact that the customers who come to fast-food restaurants *enjoy eating hamburgers and French fries.* In writing a thesis sentence, then, you should look for a controlling idea which can be effectively and easily developed within the space limitations of an essay.

Step 3: *Organize the essay.* Once you have selected a topic and written a thesis sentence expressing a controlling idea, you are ready to begin planning the development of the essay—that is, to select a method of development and to write an outline for the body paragraphs of the essay. As we pointed out earlier in this chapter, a paragraph can be looked upon as an essay in miniature. Just as every paragraph has a method of development for its supporting sentences, so every essay has a method of development for its body paragraphs. In expanding a paragraph into an essay, you did not have to worry about selecting a method of development because you were able to use the method employed in the paragraph itself. In writing an essay from scratch, however, you have to choose a method of development. You have at your disposal the same six methods which were available to you when you wrote individual paragraphs: example, definition, comparison and contrast, classification and division, cause and effect, and process analysis.

As in the case of paragraphs, you should pick the method of development which *best* develops your controlling idea. The chances are that when you picked your topic and wrote a thesis sentence about it, you had an idea of which method of development was most appropriate. If, for example, you had decided upon the thesis sentence "Of the different types of customers who frequent fast-food restaurants, some are more welcome than others," more than likely the various types of customers you have observed in fast-food restaurants inspired your topic and your thesis sentence. When you thought about the fast-food customers you had watched, in other words, you placed them in categories according to certain characteristics—that is, you classified them. As a result, you now find that the best method for developing your thesis sentence is the one you had in mind from the start—*informal classification.* However, to be certain that your original choice of method is in fact the best, you should run through the list of methods of development, from example through process analysis, and check to see whether any other method might offer a more effective way to develop your thesis sentence. Probably you will decide to stick with your first choice, but at the very least a last-minute look at the other methods will make you more confident in the choice you have made.

After you have selected a method of development, you are ready to begin the second stage in the process of organizing your essay: preparing an outline for the body paragraphs. Since writing an essay involves coordinating ideas that appear in several paragraphs, writers generally find that they need an outline to enable them to map out the overall structure of the essay. An outline serves, too, as a means of checking that structure for unity and coherence. To be effective, an outline does not need to be elaborate. It should simply remind you of the major divisions of the controlling idea which the body paragraphs will take up. It is usually sufficient, in fact, to insert a word or a phrase in the outline to represent each topic sentence and each primary-support sentence you plan to include in the body paragraphs. In short, you need not be elaborate to write an effective outline. The outline is purely for your benefit when you fill in the body paragraphs of the essay. It is a way of allowing you to see the overall pattern of your thinking and to check for problems in unity and coherence.

To prepare an outline for the body paragraphs of a 1-3-1 essay, simply write down the thesis sentence and list the three major divisions in the order in which you will discuss them. If, for instance, you were writing an essay on the thesis sentence "Of the different types of customers who frequent fast-food restaurants, some are more welcome than others," your outline might look like the following:

Thesis Sentence: Of the different types of customers who frequent fast-food restaurants, some are more welcome than others.

1. The impatient customer
2. The picky customer
3. The pleasant customer

Since the method of development you have chosen for the essay is informal classification, each of the body paragraphs in your essay should deal with a particular type of customer who eats at fast-food restaurants. The three items you've listed in the outline, therefore, represent the three classes of customer your essay will consider.

To complete your outline, you should fill in the facts and ideas you plan to use as the primary supports for the topic sentences in the body paragraphs of your essay. Again, you don't have to be elaborate. A word or a phrase is usually adequate reminder of each primary point you plan to discuss. The following outline, for example, would be appropriate for an essay on the types of customers who frequent fast-food establishments:

Thesis Sentence: Of the different types of customers who frequent fast-food restaurants, some are more welcome than others.

1. The impatient customer
   a. demands instant service
   b. angrily summons manager
   c. storms out, upsetting other customers
2. The picky customer
   a. asks for specially prepared food
   b. often returns the order
   c. expects restaurant to be run according to his whims
3. The pleasant customer
   a. asks only that the food be hot and fresh
   b. is complimentary and courteous
   c. understands delays

As a final check for unity and coherence, you might find it useful to review your outline carefully before you go on to the next step. In reviewing your outline, make sure that each of the major divisions in the essay follows the method of development you have chosen for the essay and that the divisions relate directly to the thesis sentence.

Step 4: *Furnish topic sentences for the body paragraphs of the essay.* With your outline constructed, you are ready to begin the process of filling in the essay. Before you begin writing the body of the essay, however, you need to furnish a topic sentence for each of the body paragraphs. If you have constructed your outline carefully, this step should pose little difficulty. The topic sentence of each of the body paragraphs should support the thesis sentence of the essay in the same way that the sentences of primary support develop the topic sentence in a paragraph. In other words, they should relate directly to the thesis sentence, and the evidence they present should show that the controlling idea in the thesis sentence is valid.

Thus, if you were writing an essay on fast-food customers, you would examine the three major entries in the outline and come up with topic sentences like the following:

1. The impatient customer is the most difficult type of customer for employees of fast-food restaurants to tolerate.
2. Employees in fast-food restaurants also dread waiting on the customer who is picky about what he eats and where he eats it.
3. Fortunately, however, many of the customers who frequent fast-food restaurants are easy to please and a pleasure to serve.

Each of these sentences supports the thesis sentence of the essay, and in the final draft of the essay, these sentences would become topic sentences for the body paragraphs.

Step 5: *Write the body paragraphs of the essay, and furnish a paragraph of introduction and a paragraph of conclusion.* To begin the final step, write the body paragraphs of the essay. As we noted at the beginning of this chapter, the body paragraphs of an essay often conclude with a sentence that serves as a bridge between the paragraph in which it appears and the one which follows. In furnishing the body paragraphs for the essay you are writing now, refer to your outline for the ideas and evidence you chose for your sentences of primary support. Write out the primary supports, and fill in secondary supports as needed.

When you have completed the body paragraphs of the essay, go back to the beginning of the essay and prepare an introductory paragraph; then go to the end of the essay and write a concluding paragraph. In writing introductory and concluding paragraphs, follow the same procedures you used when you wrote the introductory and concluding paragraphs for essays expanded from paragraphs. Keep in mind that an introductory paragraph should (1) state the thesis of the essay, (2) introduce the divisions in the body paragraphs of the essay, and (3) gain the reader's interest; and that a concluding paragraph should (1) restate the thesis and divisions of the essay and (2) bring the essay to a smooth close without digressing into any new issues. Before writing introductory and concluding paragraphs, then, you should review the devices at your disposal for gaining the reader's interest and for bringing your essay to a satisfying close (see pages 158–163).

Thus, a final version of the essay on fast-food customers could read as follows:

> Fast-food restaurants are becoming more and more popular in the United States. The rapid pace of contemporary society and the need of those "on the go" for quick meals bring the American public through the doors of fast-food restaurants in ever-increasing numbers. No longer is the fast-food restaurant primarily a hangout for teenagers. On the contrary, during recent years people of all ages have come to rely on

fast-food outlets as a means of satisfying their appetite for the all-American meal of hamburger, French fries, and soft drink. Playing host to such a mass of hungry drop-ins is bound to put a strain on those who work in a fast-food restaurant. Of the different types of customers who frequent fast-food restaurants, some are more welcome than others. In particular, three types of customers become very familiar to those who must serve them: the impatient ones, the picky ones, and—perhaps the salvation of the employees—the easy-to-please ones.

The impatient customer is the most difficult type of customer for employees of fast-food restaurants to tolerate. Such a customer resents having to wait at all and, while standing in line, may rattle the staff behind the counter by making angry demands for instant service. If the employees cannot meet these insistent demands, the customer may summon the manager—who may not be able to handle the customer either. An impatient customer who becomes irritated enough may walk out of the restaurant, leaving a bag or a platter of food on the table or on the counter. He may go as far as to threaten never to return to the restaurant again—often to the relief of the employees and the other customers, who have been watching the goings-on in dismay. Even if he makes good on his threat, of course, other impatient customers will come along, as will those customers who belong in the second category —the picky, or fussy, ones.

Employees in fast-food restaurants also dread waiting on the customer who is picky about what he eats and where he eats it. Because hamburgers cooked the normal way are either *too* rare or *too* well done to suit the picky customer's refined tastes, he may, for instance, put in an order for a burger "medium rare, slightly browned on one side" with "half the usual amount of ketchup, no mustard, no onions, two slices of tomato instead of one, and a dash of Worcestershire sauce to be added when the hamburger is precisely half-cooked." Even after he is given special considerations of all sorts, though, the picky customer is likely to return an order just for the sake of being able to inspect it a second time—and, perhaps, for the pleasure of being able to annoy the staff. The fussy customer seems to expect, in fact, that the restaurant be run according to his whims: utensils washed and dried with extra care, tables and floors swept or wiped two or three times during his stay— there is no end to the demands the picky customer may make. Surely, the fewer such patrons the staff has to deal with, the better. After waiting on both impatient and picky customers all day, members of the staff are probably wondering whether the job is worth all the heartache that serving such customers entails.

Fortunately, however, many of the customers who frequent fast-food restaurants are easy to please and a pleasure to serve. Pleasant customers demand little from the restaurant and its employees except that the food be hot and fresh. And pleasant customers may actually go out of their way to make an employee's job a little easier. They may compliment the staff on the neat appearance of the restaurant or on the polite and friendly service. They accept delays and are satisfied with the food as it is ordinarily prepared. Such customers compensate for the impatient and the picky and make working in a fast-food outlet more pleasant.

The recent increase in the popularity of fast-food restaurants has brought a variety of customers through the doors of local drive-in hamburger spots. Restaurant employees, feeling the pressure of working fast and nonstop, of preparing special orders, and of trying to keep everyone satisfied, have come to identify three types. Two—the impatient and the fussy—make a difficult job much more so. The third type—the pleasant customer—makes a difficult job a little easier.

SUMMARY

1. If you understand the structure of a 1-3-1 essay and can effectively expand a paragraph into a 1-3-1 essay, you should have little trouble writing this type of essay from scratch.

2. To write a 1-3-1 essay from scratch, follow these five basic steps:
   a. Select a topic.
   b. Write a thesis sentence.
   c. Organize the essay.
   d. Furnish topic sentences for the body paragraphs of the essay.
   e. Write the body paragraphs of the essay, and furnish a paragraph of introduction and a paragraph of conclusion.

3. In selecting a topic for an essay, use the same criteria which you used when selecting a topic for a paragraph. In order to write effectively about a topic, you need to be familiar with it, either from personal experience or from reading, watching television, and so on.

4. If you are assigned a topic, be sure to narrow it down sufficiently to make it manageable within the space of an essay.

5. When writing a thesis sentence for an essay, be sure the thesis statement (or sentence) expresses a controlling idea that is neither too broad nor too specific to be developed effectively.

6. To organize an essay, select a method of development and write a basic outline for the essay.

7. Often you will decide upon the method of development you want to use when you select your topic and write your thesis sentence. To make sure that you have chosen the best method available for developing your thesis sentence, check through the other methods before you finally settle on one.

8. In writing an outline, begin by listing the major divisions which the body paragraphs in your essay will discuss; then fill in the

primary supports that each body paragraph of the essay will contain. The entries in your outline need not be elaborate. Generally, a word or a phrase for each topic sentence and each primary support sentence will be sufficient.

8. For each body paragraph, furnish a topic sentence that directly relates to the thesis sentence and that is developed by the primary supports of the paragraph.

9. When writing introductory and concluding paragraphs, follow the same procedure that you used for writing introductions and conclusions to essays based on individual paragraphs. Keep in mind that an introductory paragraph should (1) state the thesis of the essay, (2) introduce the divisions in the body paragraphs of the essay, and (3) gain the interest of the reader. A concluding paragraph should (1) restate the thesis and divisions of the essay and (2) bring the essay to a smooth close without digressing into new issues.

EXERCISES

I. Narrow each of the following general subject areas (**A–G**) down to six different topics suitable for 1-3-1 essays. Follow the model given for *student life.*

Model: Student life
   1. Final examinations
   2. Living off campus
   3. Coed dormitories
   4. Intramural sports
   5. Campus activities
   6. Fraternity/sorority parties

   A. Music

   B. Health

   C. Fashions

   D. Drugs

   E. Films

   F. Automobiles

   G. Education

II. Read the following sentences and identify which ones would make good thesis sentences, which ones are too narrowly focused for discussion within the framework of a 1-3-1 essay, and which ones are too broadly focused.

A. At different stages in our lives we regard Santa Claus differently.

B. One reindeer, in particular, was Santa's favorite.

C. Santa Claus is based on a number of myths and legends about both real and fictitious people.

D. The computer center is really great.

E. The computer center was constructed for one principal purpose.

F. The computer center on campus should have been built in a more convenient location.

G. The life of a professional bowler can be extremely monotonous.

H. A recent poll showed that most men wear size eleven bowling shoes.

I. Hard-soled shoes are not permitted on bowling lanes.

J. The new tennis court is finally finished.

K. The new tennis court is unique.

L. The new tennis court is surrounded by a twelve-foot fence.

M. "Love," in tennis, means "no score."

N. The word "love" has many definitions.

O. There are many different types of discrimination.

P. Discrimination is the source of many recurrent social problems.

Q. Despite significant gains made during the turbulent sixties, discrimination is still alive and still horrible.

R. Soap operas are fun.

S. Soap operas are successful for a variety of reasons.

T. Most soap operas are on television between the hours of 1:00 and 4:00 P.M.

III. Write *one* thesis sentence for each of the following topics. Feel free to narrow the topics in whatever way you think best.

Model: Topic: Student evaluations of the faculty

Thesis: There are several reasons why student evaluations of the faculty are important.

A. *Topic:* Cheerleaders

B. *Topic:* Blizzards

C. *Topic:* Teenage pregnancy

    D. *Topic:* Intramural sports

    E. *Topic:* An embarrassing accident

    F. *Topic:* Drive-in movies

    G. *Topic:* Health spas

IV. Write an outline for an essay based on one of the following thesis sentences.

Model:

    Thesis sentence: Tourists visit vacation resorts for various reasons.

    1. Socializing

        a. meet different types of people from different backgrounds

        b. enjoy outings with other families

        c. girls meet boys (and vice versa)

    2. Activities

        a. sports

        b. amusement parks

        c. nightspots

    3. Escape

        a. get away from family

        b. break away from daily routines

        c. get away from cities

    A. Thesis sentence: Having to take basic courses in order to graduate from college can often be very frustrating.

    B. Thesis sentence: Babysitting is a good job for a teenager to consider.

    C. Thesis sentence: Living in the country is better than living in the city.

    D. Thesis sentence: Several factors indicate that the world may be on the verge of a major war.

V. Write topic sentences for each of the body paragraphs you outlined in exercise IV. Base your sentences on the notes in your outlines.

VI. Write a 1-3-1 essay based on your outline for the thesis sentence in exercise IV. When you begin writing, be sure to use the topic sentences which you wrote in exercise V for the body paragraphs of the essay.

VII. Write a 1-3-1 essay on *one* of the following thesis sentences.

A. Modern society is sold on the idea that the "new and improved" product is automatically the best.

B. A woman's place is (is not) in the home.

C. There are many different ways of coping with the monotony of everyday jobs.

D. People today place their faith in many things besides religion.

E. The seasons of the year no longer control human activities in the way that they once did.

F. Physical discipline is good (bad) for children.

G. Money doesn't buy as much as it used to.

H. Some women who think they are liberated actually are not.

I. Modern standards of heroism are so vaguely defined that the hero in one movie (or television program) could easily be the villain in another.

J. You can tell a great deal about an instructor from the way he or she walks into class.

K. Despite the many services and products it offers, the supermarket will never match the convenience and charm of the old-fashioned country store.

L. Where a student chooses to sit in a classroom may reveal several facets of his or her personality.

M. Pornography has become a multimillion-dollar business.

N. You can tell a New Englander (Southerner, Westerner, Texan, etc.) by the way he or she talks.

O. There is evidence to suggest that the theories of Dr. Benjamin Spock have done more to determine the future of American society than the work of our diplomats and political leaders.

P. Grades have lost much of the meaning they once had.

VIII: Write a 1-3-1 essay on *one* of the following topics. Feel free to narrow the topics in whatever way you think best.

A. role models

B. UFOs

C. monotony

D. talk shows

E. sex symbols

F. courtesy

G. billboards

   H. natural disasters

   I. phobias

   J. slang

   K. traffic problems

   L. health hazards

   M. civil defense

   N. condominiums

   O. the armed forces

   P. professional sports

   Q. the draft

IX. Write an essay on a topic of your own choosing. When you write the essay, be sure to follow the five steps we have given for writing a 1-3-1 essay from scratch.

Chapter 7

Revision

Even the most experienced writers recognize that their first drafts are rarely perfect and that writing good expository prose often involves careful revision. They know that in order to make their work read as smoothly and clearly as they expect it to, they must revise: that is, go over their writing word by word, sentence by sentence, paragraph by paragraph and make whatever improvements are needed. In revising, they look for problems in unity, organization, and coherence, as well as errors in mechanics such as misspelled words, faulty subject-verb agreement, and so on.

Student writers, too, must revise for the same purposes. By going over your papers for problems in unity, organization, and coherence, you can spot and correct difficulties which you may have overlooked when you first put pen to paper. You may, for example, notice that a topic sentence could be supported more effectively if its primary and secondary supports were arranged differently. Or you may, after giving your paper a final check, notice that it would be far more coherent if more transitional devices were added to smooth the flow from one sentence to the next. Revising offers you the opportunity, too, to check your work carefully for mechanical errors that you may have overlooked as you wrote.

If in writing your first draft you have applied the principles of writing that we have discussed, revision should be a relatively simple task for you. Following the step-by-step directions should have helped you avoid some of the snags that writers often run into. If, on the other hand, you find yourself making such extensive changes that the final product scarcely resembles the original version at all, you may not have followed the writing steps as carefully as you should have. Perhaps, for example, you did not select a method of development and a pattern of organization and apply them consistently throughout, or perhaps you did not furnish adequate primary and secondary support for your controlling ideas. If you find yourself in this position, it may be a good idea for you to review the steps in the writing process so that in your next composition you will be able to cover all the steps as you write the first draft, and any errors you make will be relatively minor ones: the omission of a secondary support, the substitution of a pronoun for a noun, and the like.

Although many of the concerns you have when you revise are similar to those you had when you wrote the first draft, writing and revising differ in one important respect. When you write, you are concentrating on getting your ideas down—that is, in expressing thoughts, opinions, and facts in words, sentences, and paragraphs. In your effort to include all the ideas you had planned to cover and, at the same time, to apply the principles of writing we have discussed, you may not have expressed every point as clearly as you would like to. When you revise, you have the opportunity to check your phrasing and word choice and to restate your ideas in clearer or more precise language where necessary. Revising offers you the opportunity, too, to make sure that you have arranged your ideas and facts in the most logical and effective order.

In any event, it is important to remember that the ability to revise your work successfully indicates that you have gained a grasp of the writing process. While it is surely desirable to express your ideas clearly and smoothly in the first draft, if in revising you can catch errors you have made—in structure, in phrasing, in word choice, in mechanics—you have taken a significant step toward becoming a skillful writer. As we noted before, even professional writers revise, and sometimes quite extensively.

For most student writers, revising a paper takes place in two stages. The first stage occurs after you have completed the first draft of the paper and before you arrive at what you consider the final product. The second stage occurs when you receive your work back from the instructor with suggestions on how your writing can be improved. Both stages are important, and you may find yourself making major or minor changes—or both—at either stage in the revision process. Generally, when you write a paper, you should allow yourself enough time to go over it at leisure before you give it to your instructor. To revise effectively, most writers need to distance themselves from their work so that they can approach it objectively when they begin revising. A good night's rest or a few hours of relaxation usually provide enough time for a writer to generate the mental distance necessary for effective revision. Then, when you sit down to revise, you should try to feel as though you are reading someone else's work. If you achieve this frame of mind, you will be in a position to be objective about what you have written, and you will be ready to begin revising your paper.

The first stage in the revision process, the one which takes place after you have completed the first draft of the paper, demands a rigorous examination of the paper in terms of the principles of effective writing. The way to approach this stage is to retrace the steps in the writing process. To help you in revising your work, we have devised a checklist. It consists of a series of steps involving questions which you should ask yourself as you revise. Each of the steps corresponds to a stage in the writing process. If you answer each question and revise your work where necessary, you should be able to catch any major problems in your writing before you complete the final draft, and the result will be a clearer, more effective piece of writing. Steps 1 through 4 apply to individual paragraphs, steps 5 through 7 apply to essays, and steps 8 and 9 apply to all types of compositional work.

A Checklist for Revision

Step 1: *Check the topic sentence of every paragraph.*

    a. Does the paragraph have a clearly stated topic sentence?

    b. Is the controlling idea properly focused—neither too general nor too specific for effective development?

Step 2: *Examine your paragraph for unity.*

    a. Does the paragraph contain enough primary support to develop its controlling idea effectively?

    b. Does each point of primary support have enough secondary support to develop it effectively?

    c. Does each primary support relate directly to the controlling idea of the paragraph?

    d. Does each secondary support relate directly to a primary support?

Step 3: *Check the method of development in each paragraph.*

    a. Which method of development did you select when you wrote the paragraph?

    b. Is it the method of development best suited to your topic sentence?

    c. Did you stick to that one method of development throughout the paragraph?

    d. Check the section in this book on the method of development you have chosen, and make sure that you have developed the paragraph according to the directions given there.

Step 4: *Examine your paragraphs for coherence.*

    a. What pattern of organization do the primary and secondary supports in your paragraph follow: time order, space order, or order of importance?

    b. Check the section in this book on the pattern of organization you have used, and make sure you have followed the instructions there.

    c. Are the ideas and the sentences in your paragraphs smoothly connected?

    d. Have you included sufficient transitional words and phrases between ideas and sentences?

    e. Are the transitional words and phrases you have selected appropriate and effective?

    f. Have you avoided the awkward repetition of nouns by replacing some of them with pronouns?

    g. Is the tense of the verbs in each paragraph consistent throughout the paragraph?

Step 5: *Check the introductory paragraph of your essay.*

    a. What device did you use to gain the attention of your reader? Do you think that this device will be successful in stimulating reader interest?

    b. Does the introductory paragraph of your essay state the thesis of the essay?

    c. Is the thesis one which can be developed effectively in a short essay?

    d. Does the introductory paragraph of your essay state the divisions to be developed in the body paragraphs of the essay?

Step 6: *Check the body paragraphs of every essay.*

    a. Does each body paragraph begin with a topic sentence?

    b. Does the topic sentence of each body paragraph support the thesis of the essay?

    c. Is there adequate transition between body paragraphs?

    d. Does each body paragraph follow the principles of unity, organization, and coherence specified in steps 2 through 4 of this checklist?

Step 7: *Check the concluding paragraph of every essay.*

    a. What device did you use to bring your essay to a close?

    b. Did you restate your essay's thesis and division in different words?

    c. Does the device you used bring the essay to a smooth close without introducing any new facts or ideas? Does the conclusion provide your reader with a sense of completion?

Step 8: *Examine your paragraphs for mechanical errors.*

    a. Is every sentence in each paragraph a complete sentence?

    b. Does every sentence end with a terminal punctuation mark?

    c. Are the clauses and phrases in your sentences properly punctuated?

    d. Do the subjects of your clauses and sentences agree in number with their verbs?

    e. Are the pronouns in your paragraph in the proper case?

    f. If your work contains quotation marks, dashes, colons, or parentheses, are they used correctly?

    g. Does your work contain any misplaced modifiers?

    h. Does your work contain any dangling modifiers?

    i. Are all the words in your work spelled correctly?

Step 9: *Finally, give your paragraph or essay a last, quick reading.*

SUMMARY

1. Most writers agree that the best expository prose is arrived at by a process of careful revision.

2. Revision of a paragraph or an essay takes place in two stages. The first stage occurs after you have completed the first draft of the paper; the second stage takes place after your instructor returns the paper to you with suggestions for improvement.

3. During the first stage in the revision process, you should check through your work to make sure that it is free from structural and mechanical problems and to see if there are any ways in which your writing can be strengthened and improved.

4. To revise your work effectively, you should put away your writing until enough time has elapsed for you to approach the revision process objectively.

5. As a guide to revision, follow the checklist above.

EXERCISES

I. Using the checklist for revision on pp. 185–187, revise the following paragraphs:

    A. There are six ways to reduce one's chances of having a heart attack. One of the most important of these is to reduce the amount of saturated fat and cholesterol in one's diet. For example, cooking should be done with polyunsaturated shortening. Also, the amount of eggs and whole-milk dairy products can be strictly limited. Another way to avoid trouble is to keep trim. Life expectancy is longer for men and women who maintain a reasonable weight. Dieting may be necessary to be sure that they do not put on extra pounds. Another important safeguard against heart attack is regular exercise. People who have sedentary jobs and who do not make an effort to get regular exercise are much more susceptible to heart attacks than are people whose jobs involve physical activity or who engage in sports or jog to stay fit. Smoking leads to heart attacks. The government should ban tobacco as being very harmful to health. If tobacco is not banned, people will continue to smoke because the average man or woman lacks enough self-discipline to keep from smoking. People can reduce the risk of heart attack by following these simple rules for maintaining a strong heart and a healthy cardiovascular system.

    B. Medicaid is a government-supported insurance program that is used by many Americans. Since Medicaid pays for a patient's treatment while in an emergency room, some Medicaid patients think nothing of going to an emergency room for the treatment of minor ailments like colds and coughs. Since the basic fee for an emergency room is $34.00 and the basic fee for the average office visit is $15.00, patients who come to the emergency room to receive treatment that could just as easily be administered in a doctor's office drive up the cost of the Medicaid program for the taxpayer. They tie up the facilities of the emergency room for people who really need them. Because doctors also earn more for treating patients in an emergency room, many physicians refuse to stop Medicaid patients from coming to the emergency room when these patients could be treated elsewhere. Most private insurance companies will not cover clinical emergency services. The American tax dollar, in the form of Medicaid, will come to the aid of patients who abuse the program.

    C. Striving too hard to win may be the greatest mistake a person can make. When a person sets a goal and then concentrates on nothing but that goal, he loses the little things in life. For example, a boy playing in a school football team finds the pressure to win, to reach that goal, the most important thing in his life. It is important not only to him but to the coach and teammates, and to his friends and his family. The pressure can result in a boy concentrating on nothing else but to win at playing football. He forgets the fun of the game and the good times he could have doing other activities. Grown people act this way in business, where to reach an economic goal is so strong that they will even step on friends in order to obtain a higher status in life. When one sets a goal, they should be willing to except a setback or even a failure in their social life.

D. Some indication that the American people are at last finding, exploring, and expressing their individuality is clearly evident in the way they dress. If you follow the history of fashion you will find that Americans used to drool in anticipation over what is being "shown" in Paris or Rome. Simply agonizing over whether they can afford just one fashionable garment. The broad middle class goes their own way and people reveal their self-chosen role in society through the cloths they wear. Today's clothing depicts many different lifestyles. From the 1920s to the 1970s, styles changed in America. People today can wear any style popular during previous decades and feel comfortable. Today you sometimes see full skirts and peasant blouses. Or you may see a dress inspired by "flapper" dresses of the twenties. This was the era of short skirts and the Charleston. You may see saddle oxfords reminiscent of the thirties and forties, along with patent-leather plumps in low-, medium-, or high-heel versions. A long-haired boy swaggers down the street in ragged jeans and a faded tee shirt, perhaps sporting a golden earring through a pierced ear. He may not realize it, but he has a sort of gypsy look. An executive goes about his daily business in his business suit. On his face is an expression of pride in what he stands for. A girl with no makeup and easy-care hair style, wearing overalls and sneakers, walks side by side with a friend with crimped hair, a made-up face, ankle-length skirt, and spiked heels. On campus all of these types and many more mill around between classes. One can even see turbans from India, the long costume of a young black America's ancestral home, boots, bumper stickers, cowboy hats, cut-off jeans, and sandles. Long hair, short hair, plaited hair—the list of hairstyles is endless. Each person wishes to achieve self-identity through dress, and dress has consequently become an important way to project one's self-image on the world.

II. Using the checklist on pp. 185–187, revise two or more paragraphs which you wrote earlier in the course.

III. Using the checklist on pp. 185–187, revise the following essays.

A. America currently faces the single most threatening crisis in its two-hundred-year history. This crisis threatens to shut down every major industry, all transportation, and the massive business of agriculture. The crisis is over energy. Energy being the life blood of the United States. Most of the disasters facing us can be avoided through proper planning and cooperation from the government, industry, and the people.

If a major energy crisis is to be averted, the government of the United States should determine the energy-saving policies which our country desperately needs. The government must design and activate a policy for conserving energy needs and resources, and this policy must take into account not only the near future but the distant future as well. Tax incentives should encourage industry, as well as the general public, to conserve the use of all energy. This form of financial leverage would exist in forms of tax breaks for power companies to find more efficient means for production of electricity. Also financing of an insulating plan for most homes and businesses would come as a must in this energy policy. One of the major parts of an energy policy would center on transportation. As of 1977, transportation in the United States used at least 27 percent of the country's total energy consumption, and this excessive consumption tends to increase yearly. With this in mind, mass transportation needs more serious study and consideration. Mass transportation needs a government boost to get such a massive project underway. Such a transportation project help the energy crunch. It would also add many thousands of jobs to a rapidly shrinking job market.

But the public should take primary responsibility for conserving energy. The government should educate the American public to the importance of conserving natural resources. It can do this through an extensive and wide-ranging educational campaign. The public needs to be taught to purchase smaller, less energy-consuming automobiles. Also, Americans will have to learn how to get around their towns without automobiles. The public must learn to curtail senseless trips like using an automobile for a four-block trip to a local grocery store. The public also needs to learn how to conserve energy in the home. Buying and using an overabundance of electrical appliances has put a great deal of strain on our energy resources. People also need to curtail the constant use of lights, air conditioners, and other high-energy appliances, and they need to lower their thermostats to 65°. Even lower, if possible, at night.

Industry, too, should be enlisted in the crusade to conserve energy in America. Along with the government and the American public, industry can help to conserve vast quantities of gas and oil. The manufacturers of energy-consuming products need to make appliances which are more efficient in the amounts of energy they use. The development of efficient automobiles or alternate energy sources would help to conserve energy greatly. Industry should consider sponsoring research into alternative sources of power such as solar power, wind energy, and geothermal heat.

To historians of the future, the next half century of American history will resound as the real test of America's strength and ingenuity. Will all the various factions in American society unite and cooperate, or will they all collapse together? Only time will tell.

B. The traditional American funeral has been called a social function at which the deceased is the guest of honor. Approximately 22,500 funeral establishments in the United States compete to bury two million bodies a year. Next to buying a house or a car, purchasing a funeral is the largest single investment a person is likely to make in his lifetime. The average funeral is likely to cost more than two thousand dollars, and the funeral industry itself is a thriving multimillion-dollar business. Perhaps people should think twice before they decide to bury their dead in the way the funeral industry tells us the dead should be buried. Knowing the facts about such costly funeral items and services as caskets, embalming, and graveyard plots can put you at a decided advantage should you ever have to confront a funeral director and purchase these things for someone you love.

The casket is the single most expensive item on the funeral bill. The object of good casket salesmanship is encouraging you to spring for the higher price models. A substantial percentage of your final payment may wind up in the salesman's pocket. In an attempt to cater to and encourage the American mania for luxury items, manufacturers have produced caskets of a wide variety of materials. They offer them in glass, steel, wood, cement, marble, rubber, and even plastic. Whatever one decides to buy in the way of a casket, you should remember one thing: you will not be around to see what you look like in it. And your friends will only have an hour or so to admire your choice before it disappears in the ground encased in two thousand pounds of concrete and covered with half a ton of dirt. Something of a cross between a bed and a bomb shelter, your casket is your home for eternity. But who, including you, will remember what it looked like or how much it cost?

Embalming is also a costly item on the funeral bill, but is not as necessary a service as you may think. You are not required by law to be embalmed unless you have succumbed to a contagious disease. Too grisly to describe in detail, embalming is a process most people might be well to do without. Technically it is simply the replacing of bodily fluids with a liquid preservative, but when it comes to actual methods, suffice it to say that you are lucky that you are dead when they do it to you. More and more people are beginning to think that embalming is a senseless waste of time and money, an expensive luxury that can raise the price of a funeral by as much as two hundred dollars.

Another item on the funeral bill is the cemetery plot. Depending on their location, you can buy a cemetery plot from anywhere from a hundred to several hundred dollars. You also need, in some states, some type of vault to hold the casket when it is placed in the ground. Cemetery plots can be purchased from the funeral director or from the cemetery people themselves. The cost of a cemetery plot usually depends on the social status of the cemetery where it is located. Exclusive cemeteries which cater to the wealthy resemble spacious parks, and the plots are quite expensive. Older, less exclusive cemeteries sell you plots for much lower prices.

A final note with regard to another costly aspect of funerals: the social aspect. Many homes involved in a funeral are taxed to overflowing with guests who must be fed and, sometimes, housed at motels, often at the expense of the family involved. A funeral should not be a festive occasion. And it should not become more of a financial burden because of large food bills incurred in the feeding of countless guests.

In short, funerals should not be as expensive as they are. Until people decide what they want for the bodies of their dead, American funerals will continue to be a mysterious and expensive rite. According to Mary Hartman, "there should be a new field of funeral people who are much less funereal.

... The way they do it now is just much too serious. It should be sillier or something ... maybe they should play games."

IV. Using the chart on pp. 185–187, revise an essay which you wrote for one of the exercises in Chapter 6.

Revising a Graded Paper

The second stage in the revision process takes place when you have received your paper back from your instructor. More than likely your paper, even if it is a good one, will contain suggestions for improvement, and you may be asked to revise it in the light of these comments. If you reworked your paper carefully during the first stage of the revision process, the changes your instructor recommends may be fairly minor. You may be asked, for example, to add, delete, or change punctuation marks or to correct a misspelled word. Or if your paper needs more transitional devices, you may be asked to insert them where your instructor feels they are necessary.

However, if you did not write your paper carefully, you may find that even at this late stage your paper requires more radical revision than the addition of a comma or the correction of a misspelled word. Your instructor may feel, for instance, that a paragraph needs additional primary or secondary support or that the facts or ideas you have chosen as support can be emphasized or clarified by a reorganization of your material. Whatever suggestions, major or minor, your instructor gives you for revision, you should consider them carefully, for they constitute an evaluation of your writing from the vantage point of an observant and highly trained reader. Not only do the suggestions you receive point the way to an improvement of the work you have handed in, but they are also likely to tell you which aspects of the writing process you should devote more attention to in the future.

Editors and instructors use a more or less standardized list of symbols and abbreviations for indicating the necessity for certain types of revision. The symbols and abbreviations most instructors and readers use are shown in Figure 7-1. In addition to using some of the symbols and abbreviations listed in Figure 7-1, your instructor may make a more detailed comment in the margin of your paper or at the beginning or end of the paper.

In revising a paper, you should interpret the remarks of your instructor and then make the appropriate changes. Consider the following paragraph:

The English names of the days of the week honor the

sp/ two most prominent (heavily) bodies, four germanic deities, /*cap* /*n*

agr/ and one Roman god. Sunday and Monday (is) named for the

(delete)	delete	_awk_	awkward wording
∧/∨	add omitted word(s)	_wdy_	wordy
_sp_	check spelling	_cap_	change to capital letter
¶	begin new paragraph	_lc_	change to lower-case letter
vag	vague	_incoh_	incoherent
∼	transpose order	_ital_	italicize
∧	insert period	;/	insert semicolon
:/	insert colon	∧	insert comma
∨	insert apostrophe	∨	insert quotation marks
no ¶	no new paragraph	[_frag_]	fragment
_cs_	comma splice	_ro_	run-on sentence
⟨?⟩	insert question mark	⟨!⟩	insert exclamation point
wdc	check choice of word(s)	_agr_	check agreement
vbt	check verb tense	_dev_	develop further
_ex_	give example	_mis mod_	misplaced modifier
dang	dangling modifier	⊂	close up
?	meaning is unclear	_amb_	ambiguous
cliché	trite word or expression	_Trans_ ∧	add transition
S	faulty sentence structure	_not //_	check parallelism

Figure 7-1

wdc/ sun and moon, (respectfully) Tuesday, Wednesday, Thurs-
day, and Friday honor Teutonic gods. Tuesday is Tiw's day ⊙ /_cs_
Trans / the name ∧ honors the German ᶦᶜ god of war. Wednesday is /_Cap_
∨ / Woden's day. [Woden being the god of magic, wisdom, and [_frag_]
Can you develop further being a warrior god also.] Thursday is named for the thun-
the significance of the two warrior gods? der god Thor. Friday is probably named for the goddess
Frig ∧ the wife of Woden. [Though Frig may have been con- /∧ [_frag_]
fused with Freya.] Saturday is named for the Roman God /_lc_
dev / Saturnus, or Saturn, as he is sometimes called. Saturday,
then, is Saturn's day, and it completes the cycle that began
with Sunday.

This paragraph has been marked for correction and is ready to be
revised. The revision of the paragraph follows:

The English names of the days of the week honor the two most
prominent heavenly bodies, four Germanic deities, and one Roman
god. Sunday and Monday are named for the sun and moon, respectively.
Tuesday, Wednesday, Thursday, and Friday honor Teutonic gods. Tuesday is Tiw's day; the name of this day honors the Germanic god of war.

Wednesday is Woden's day. Woden was the Germanic god of magic and wisdom. Like Tiw, he was also a warrior, and the fact that two days of the week are named after gods of war is an indication of the importance of war in early Germanic culture. Thursday is named for the thunder god Thor. Friday is probably named for the goddess Frig, the wife of Woden, although it may have been named for Freya, the Scandinavian goddess of fertility. Saturday is named for the Roman god Saturnus, or Saturn, as he is sometimes called. Saturday, then, is Saturn's day, and it completes the cycle which began with Sunday.

In this paragraph, the writer has used the suggestions which she received from her instructor on her original draft as the basis for her revisions. The result is a clearer, more coherent paragraph that has benefited greatly from the revision it has received.

SUMMARY

1. The second stage in the revision process takes place when you have received your paper from your instructor, who has marked it with suggestions as to how it can be improved.
2. The chart on p. 194 lists the kinds of marks and symbols instructors and editors use when evaluating a piece of writing.
3. When you receive a graded paper back from your instructor, refer to the chart in order to determine the revisions which your instructor feels you should make.

EXERCISES

I. Take one of the graded paragraphs you wrote for Chapters 4 or 5 and revise it according to the suggestions made by your instructor.

II. Take one of the graded essays you wrote for Chapter 6 and revise it according to the suggestions made by your instructor.

Index